ADVANCE PRAISE FOR *MORAL LEADERSHIP*

"*Moral Leadership* by Chaplain (MAJ) Jim Linzey shows the military, the common person, executives, and the clergy how to lead on the job or at home. Linzey pulls no punches in dealing with leadership, professionalism, or integrity."
—*Rear Admiral Bennett S. Sparks, USCG-Ret.*
Former Secretary General, Congress of International Reservists
(Chartered by NATO)

"Chaplain Jim Linzey has captured the thoughts that are essential for leadership, both in the military and in the corporate world. Our nation yearns to have good solid men and women of character who can influence others. Leadership is all about people and Chaplain Linzey's book will be helpful to all of us as we seek to make a difference in the lives of others and have an impact on our nation."
—*Brigadier General Dick Abel, USAF (Ret.)*
Former Executive Director, Military Ministry, Campus Crusade for Christ

"Chaplain (Major) Jim Linzey uniquely captures the vital components of being an effective leader in any venue applicable to a variety of circumstances. He builds the moral, ethical, and God-centered foundation of leadership coupled to the technical aspects of developing leadership skills and then gives us lessons on how to become responsible, resourceful, competent, and influential leaders."
—*Rear Admiral Paul K. Arthur, USNR (Ret.)*
Former Technical Director & Deputy to the Commanding General
White Sands Missile Range, New Mexico

"I have been a leader of men for thirty-eight years. However, this book has provided insights and material that will certainly enhance and broaden my future efforts. I am certain that Chaplain Linzey's book will impact the lives of all who seek competency to lead. Without reservation, I highly recommend this work to all who seek to be effective leaders in their spheres of influence."
—*Dr. Ralph Bell, Former Associate Evangelist*
Billy Graham Evangelistic Association

"The interior life of the leader—expressed consciously or unconsciously—casts a variation of light or shadow throughout the organization. Jim Linzey has done his homework, aptly reminding us how the leader's character is central to team building, communication and organizational effectiveness."
—Roger Heuser, Ph.D.
Adjunct Professor, Fuller Theological Seminary
Professor of Leadership Studies,
Vanguard University of Southern California

"It is said that if you steal from one person, it's plagiarism, but from many it is called research. This book is so good I did 'research' on it (sic). He has filled it with truth, principles, stories, and a lifetime of training and practical living. It is filled with instruction, not just information. It is a 'must read' for any person in leadership. I recommend it."
—Edwin Louis Cole
Founding President, Christian Men's Network

"Jim Linzey has both studied and observed leadership at close levels. His vast experience in the military and his deeply held Christian convictions have been brought fully to bear on this vital issue for today. In our fast-changing and challenging world, those in search of the character and skills of leadership will find much helpful material to work with in his insightful book."
—Dr. Colin Dye, Senior Pastor, Kensington Temple, London City Church

"Dr. Linzey has captured in words how we can be leaders in both the secular and non-secular worlds. His practical approach and in-depth research are easily understandable and achievable. Well done, true and faithful servant."
—Rod Readhead, CEO, Promise Keepers, United Kingdom

"Linzey's book is an important reminder that leadership not only embraces what one does, but who one is. By beginning with character formation, Linzey provides readers with an opportunity to grow in their leadership abilities, regardless of their current responsibilities."
—Dr. Erin DeMeester Reynolds
Former Assistant Professor of Communications
Fuller Theological Seminary

"Dr. Linzey's book recognizes that every one of us can learn to be a leader. Leadership is an accumulation of character and habits. The most important being service—serving one another."
—The Honorable Lori Holt Pfeiler, Former Mayor of Escondido, California

Moral Leadership

Moral Leadership
The 9 Leadership Traits

JAMES F. LINZEY

RESOURCE *Publications* • Eugene, Oregon

MORAL LEADERSHIP
The 9 Leadership Traits

Copyright © 2015 James F. Linzey. All rights reserved. Except for brief quotations in critical publications or reviews, no part of this book may be reproduced in any manner without prior written permission from the publisher. Write: Permissions, Wipf and Stock Publishers, 199 W. 8th Ave., Suite 3, Eugene, OR 97401.

Resource Publications
An Imprint of Wipf and Stock Publishers
199 W. 8th Ave., Suite 3
Eugene, OR 97401

www.wipfandstock.com

ISBN 13: 978-1-4982-3316-3

Manufactured in the U.S.A.

To my mother,
Verna M. Linzey
Bible Translator, Editor, Author,
Ordained Minister, Singer, Hymn Writer,
Recording Artist

Contents

Foreword by Doug Pierce ♦ *xi*
Preface ♦ *xiii*
Acknowledgements ♦ *xv*
Introduction ♦ *xvii*

- one   Moral Leadership in the Founding of America ♦ 1
- two   The Ten Commandments as the Roots of American Culture ♦ 11
- three   The Nine Leadership Traits ♦ 21
- four   Effectiveness of the Moral Leader ♦ 72
- five   Core Values for Moral Leadership ♦ 89
- six   Team Leadership ♦ 96
- seven   Communication Under Moral Leadership ♦ 123
- eight   Character Formation as Key to Moral Leadership ♦ 133
- nine   Conclusion ♦ 147

Appendix: Personal Mission Statement ♦ *149*
Bibliography and Recommended Reading ♦ *153*
Subject Index ♦ *157*

Foreword

MORAL LEADERSHIP IS BOTH timely and timeless. The principles and practices that the author presents in this book are timeless because they are found in the Holy Bible. They are also a timely antidote to an ailing society

Readers will be both inspired and troubled by the chapters that deal with moral leadership in the founding of America and the Ten Commandments as the roots of American culture. They will be inspired as they are reminded of the moral integrity of those who founded our great nation and they will be troubled by how far we, as a nation—as a people, have fallen from those lofty principles.

Is there hope for restoration to the ideals and principles of the founding fathers? Yes, says Jim Linzey, who throughout the book draws upon the advanced formal education in leadership provided him by the United States Air Force. Jim takes these principles and distills and presents them in a way that can benefit everyone, including church leaders, corporate leaders, military leaders, and the average person.

Moral Leadership applies these principles to all spheres of influence in the world of corporations, the military, the church, and family and friends. *Moral Leadership* provides a comprehensive approach to both basic and advanced leadership principles. *Moral Leadership* equips people to be the most effective leaders they can possibly be by revolutionizing their lives with state-of-the-art leadership tools—tools to take charge, empower, and lead.

Foreword

  Some of these tools include the nine leadership traits essential to the effectiveness of a moral leader as well as the twelve principles of job leadership and the twelve habits of effective leaders. The author gets down to the nitty-gritty as he presents decision-making techniques, relationship dynamics, and authority and conflict resolution.

  Throughout the book, much emphasis is placed on character formation and its key role in moral leadership. This book reflects the character and moral stance of author Jim Linzey who served in both the United States Air Force and the United States Army where he experienced being under the leadership of others and being in the responsible position of leader to many.

  Jim Linzey's well researched and carefully crafted book on the subject of moral leadership is a must read for anyone in leadership. The principles presented in this book could transform the moral fiber of our nation. I highly recommend it.

Brigadier General Doug Pierce, USAF (Ret.)
June 2015

Preface

I BEGAN WRITING THIS manuscript in 1999 in my personal time while on active duty at Fort Lee, Virginia, as the chaplain for the largest battalion in the U.S. Army. I revised this manuscript many times over the past twelve years. My pilgrimage during these years has enriched my own understanding of leadership and enabled me to provide the reader a deeper understanding of the truths set forth in this book.

While serving in positions of leadership, I have seen how many corporate executives, commanders, clergy, and parents not only needed mentoring, but also a clearer vision of what leaders must do, and guidance on where to find the required knowledge.

While there are many excellent resources on leadership, *Moral Leadership* synthesizes what leadership is all about and prepares all leaders to begin leading right where they are. Leaders in every strata of society are in special need of help due to the cultural crises facing western civilization. Today's cultural whirlwind pressures leaders such as statesmen, churchmen, and businessmen to do the impossible task of leaving the morality out of leadership in an increasingly atheistic society. This book presents leadership skills that are applicable to every sphere of influence. These skills will be extremely beneficial to leaders who want to remain both moral and in the lead.

James F. Linzey
Escondido, California
June 2015

Acknowledgements

I AM TRULY GRATEFUL for the example of leadership that my mother, Verna M. Linzey, D.D., is and has been throughout my life. She has impacted my life more than any other person. Her example of deep spirituality, integrity, and bravery through decades of tough times has strengthened and encouraged me to excel with character throughout my entire life. My mother is an intellectual who has unequivocally placed service before her own professional endeavors, and she has influenced many organizations and individuals to succeed when they might have failed. I have gained so much knowledge at her feet, and at her bedside on my knees praying every morning before going to school, while my father, Captain Stanford E. Linzey, Jr., Chaplain Corp, United States Navy (Retired), served our nation often away at sea. I owe a tremendous debt of gratitude to my parents for the way they reared me.

Dr. Edwin Louis Cole greatly honored me when he invited me to assist him as his right-hand man in the Christian Men's Network. Circumstances related to Dr. Cole's passing away prevented us from working together. I am deeply grateful for the uplifting words he shared with me about this manuscript and the encouragement he gave me to publish it. *Moral Leadership* was the last book he endorsed.

Dr. Erin DeMeester Reynolds, former Associate Professor of Communications at Fuller Theological Seminary, has greatly encouraged me to dig deep into the meaning of communication and write about it in this book. Her insights have helped me

Acknowledgements

tremendously to make the chapter on communication and this book what it is. To her, I am truly grateful.

Lieutenant Colonel James M. Pickett, my Senior Instructor for the U.S. Army's Combined Arms and Services Staff School, not only taught me how to use decision matrices in class, he also assisted me in the formulation of the "The Decision Matrix" section in this book, so that everyone could understand it. I also appreciate him for having allowed me to give meditations at the beginning of each class, and conduct worship services prior to the beginning of his lectures on Sundays. During these memorable worship services, he, as a Roman Catholic Eucharistic minister, assisted me and other officers in serving communion.

I would like to thank my former commander, LTC David Merritt, USA (Ret.), for requesting me by name to serve as his chaplain for the largest battalion in the U.S. Army—the 244th Quartermaster Battalion, 23d Brigade, Fort Lee, Virginia. For it was there that I was motivated to write this book. And there I gave leadership seminars to the lieutenants and cadre at the Quartermaster Officers Basic Course. And while serving at Fort Lee, I was requested to conduct a Joint Military Leadership Seminar for Air Force, Army and Navy chaplains and chaplain assistants at the Armed Forces Staff College and aboard the USS Briscoe, both of which were at Naval Air Station Norfolk, Virginia.

Finally, I would like to convey my heartfelt thanks to the following for the long hours they spent assisting me by editing this manuscript: Father Michael Pacella, III, who served with my father aboard the USS *Coral Sea*; Shirley Felt, PhD, who is my former college English professor; Linda Nathan, who has graciously assisted me on a number of projects; and Carla Bruce who also served as one of my proofreaders for the Modern English Version Bible.

James F. Linzey
Escondido, California
June 2015

Introduction

ALL LEADERSHIP SKILLS ARE learned. No one has the edge over anyone else. In other words, people are born with equal abilities to lead. Leaders must have a moral compass on which to build these skills. *Moral Leadership* provides the moral compass for prospective leaders—to broaden their spheres of influence, to empower their people, and to create teamwork among their families, friends, and church or corporate staff members or co-workers. Teamwork is a necessity in accomplishing both personal and professional goals.

We are easily distracted and subject to the negative influences that surround us. Consequently, we can fall prey to these external influences, lose our vision, and become powerless—falling short of our goals. However, we can regain power over our lives by focusing on our main goals and ordering everything else around those goals. Then we can succeed in life. But that is only the beginning. To be truly influential, we should duplicate our successes in the lives of others by improving their "serve." While some leaders may think that serving others will cause them to feel like slaves, they do not understand how their subordinates perceive them. Subordinates usually perceive such leaders as heroes. The art of serving makes heroes out of ordinary people. *Moral Leadership* teaches the art of serving, which is really the art of helping others succeed and fulfill their dreams.

Servanthood begins with identifying "customers" and then attending to them. People should see everyone within their spheres of influence as their customers. A customer is anyone with whom

Introduction

one comes into contact. This outlook facilitates three things: expanding one's sphere of influence, being pleasant, and developing a competitive edge. These qualities attract new friends and employment opportunities. The best customers are repeat customers. And the best services are those that attract repeat customers. *Moral Leadership* empowers people to develop their customer base through offering *outstanding services* to those within their sphere of influence and to *expanding their sphere of influence.*

> The lack of tools prevents many leaders from serving their best; therefore, this book offers a myriad of tools to assist leaders in gaining self-esteem, confidence, and leadership skills. Shy individuals will learn to speak in public with poise and confidence. The experienced will fine-tune their Power Point presentations. Indecisiveness will wane as leaders emerge with ethical decision- making techniques, lead teams through change, and master presentations, such as speeches, sermons, information briefs, and decision briefs.

People often buy *how-to* books for short-term solutions to long-term leadership deficiencies. These books usually suggest change through the personality ethic. The *personality ethic* is "the manipulation of others into behaving in prescribed manners." It focuses on developing charisma and manipulating people to do what you want them to do—regardless of ethics—in order to be "approved." People who manipulate in this way might not realize what they are doing, and they often act out learned behaviors from their role models. Unfortunately, the result might not reflect the character ethic.

The *character ethic* is "positively influencing the behavior of others through modeling leadership traits." It focuses on developing character in others, thereby *influencing* and *directing* people to accomplish their missions in an ethical manner and to do what is right regardless of what anyone says or thinks. The personality ethic is ego-centered, while the character ethic is mission-centered. Nevertheless, charisma is a wonderful quality for leaders with character. Used wisely, charisma complements people who have character. But it can be a tool of destruction in the hands of those with manipulative agendas. Not everyone is born with charisma, though everyone may develop and nurture it. Everyone, however, is born with character and is morally responsible for maintaining and growing in it. However, character can be lost through unwise decision-making in one's personal life. *Moral Leadership* shows how to develop and maintain character. Character is indispensable in bringing out the leader in people. While leadership can be a technique for the egomaniac, it is a way of life for the morally upright.

While the personality ethic induces mere *surface alterations*, the character ethic produces *sub-surface transformations*. The character ethic is the key to lasting change because it leaves an indelible imprint on the mind. The character ethic is the modeling of leadership traits that produce change in one's behavior. As such, character is the basis of *Moral Leadership*.

Moral Leadership discusses the traits that are based on the character ethic. Significant others, friends, acquaintances, parishioners, and employees will change the way they perceive leaders who emulate these traits. *Moral Leadership* shows how to expand spheres of influence through changing one's self-concept.

For many people, change seems unnecessary unless there is something wrong with the status quo. They say, "If it's not broken, don't fix it." But when it is broken, change is required. Sound leadership knows the difference and provides a support structure to make change a reality. *Accepting* change requires *willingness*, but *adapting* to change requires *flexibility*. Good leaders provide the support structure so followers can make the changes. Growing through change is a serious, tenacious commitment to improving leadership skills at all levels.

Leading effectively requires defining the following critical issues:

- What business we are in
- What is important around us
- What and who we are as individuals

Introduction

- What and who we really want to be as individuals
- Who we are as leaders

Defining these issues enables people to lead in any strata of society and build productive working relationships.

When people experience dynamic relationships within their personal and professional spheres of influence and apply the principles to their homes and organizations on a daily basis, their lives will explode with success!

Moral Leadership applies these principles to all spheres of influence in the world of corporations, the military, the church, and family and friends. *Moral Leadership* provides a comprehensive approach to both basic and advanced leadership principles. *Moral Leadership* equips people to be the most effective leaders they can possibly be by revolutionizing their lives with state-of-the-art leadership tools—tools to take charge, empower, and lead.

Chapter 1 explores the moral basis of early American leaders and the influences undermining morality in American society. It discusses how to create a moral atmosphere in organizations. Chapter 2 presents the Ten Commandments as the basis of American Civilization. Chapter 3 defines leadership and discusses how to lead, mentor, and supervise. Chapter 4 shows how to assimilate core values into our lives at the organizational and personal levels and to identify core qualities of leadership. Chapter 5 shows how to develop one's sphere of influence and effectively direct people through ethical decision-making processes, stages of empowering people, building and maintaining teams, and fostering relationships. Chapter 6 teaches how to communicate publicly and interpersonally, and how to prepare and deliver speeches, sermons, and briefs. Chapter 7 describes character formation comprised of confession, healing the soul, sound beliefs, and unconditional acceptance. Chapter 8 summarizes the lessons learned and includes a closing statement. And, finally, the appendix provides a tool to facilitate achieving personal goals.

If you are ready to influence people and succeed in life, then I invite you to read this book.

one

Moral Leadership in the Founding of America

> The very highest leader is barely known by men.
> Then comes the leader they know and love.
> Then the leader they fear.
> Then the leader they despise.
> The leader who does not trust enough will not be trusted.
> When actions are performed without unnecessary speech,
> The people say, "We did it ourselves."
>
> —Lao Tsu

"Leadership" is a word that implies a fairly well known process. We all know what the term means—at least we think we do. In addition, most of us would agree that we know what "moral" means—at least in an amorphous, ambiguous way we do. It is, after all, a non-tangible word, and hence the definition will vary from culture to culture, from situation to situation, and even from person to person. Therefore, it is not easy to define specifically. However, this does not negate "natural law" or the existence of "universals," which are moral principles applying to everyone.

Moral Leadership

Thus, to clarify the point being made by "moral leadership," it is important to define and illustrate the terms in the ways intended in this book and this chapter.

Leadership is both a process and a set of practices. Therefore, leadership is amoral. However, leaders can use all processes and practices for either good or evil; they can be ruthless and oppressive or considerate and supportive. Therefore, it is the *use* of such processes that we associate with either morality or immorality. Leaders, on the other hand, are definitely moral or immoral, although we cannot as easily identify their actions as moral or immoral. The society under which the leader works determines whether the actions of that leader are moral or immoral. For example, authors James Kouzes and Barry Posner acknowledge that "Charles Manson may have been an insanely skillful practitioner of the art of leadership in the amoral sense of the term, but he was not a moral leader."[1] People like Manson, who lead others into paths the society they live in does not approve, have no legitimacy as moral leaders because they violate the shared values of their societies.

The true test of moral leadership, says leadership scholar James MacGregor Burns, is when a leader's actions are "grounded in conscious choice among real alternatives. Any leader who would impose his or her will upon others and allow them no choice is not morally legitimate."[2] Leaders must decide what they stand for, and they must allow their constituencies to choose their leaders based on those stands or moral judgments that the leaders stand for. Moreover, followers do want to follow those who exhibit moral leadership.

In another book by Kouzes and Posner, the authors report the results of a questionnaire they gave to several thousand business and government executives. They asked the question, "What values (personal traits or characteristics) do you look for and admire in your superiors?" The responses identified many traits, of course, but the surprising result was that the top four traits desired were

1. Kouzes and Posner, *Credibility*, 66.
2. Burns, *Leadership*, 36.

invariably the same: Executives wanted leaders to be Honest—88 percent, Forward-Looking—75 percent, Inspiring—68 percent, and Competent—63 percent.[3] Notice that the top choice had to do with the moral stance of the leaders, not the ability or knowledge we might assume would be first. This kind of result would lead us to believe that people really want moral leadership; the moral side of a leader tends to give others a sense of security.

To create high morality in any organization or group, we must hold the right values. Historically, some of the proponents of value system leadership have taken a neutral position on values clarification. Such a position has weakened the stand leaders must take. For example, Merrill Harmin states, "Our emphasis on value neutrality probably did undermine traditional morality, . . . It makes a good deal of sense to say that truthfulness is better than deception, caring is better than hurting, loyalty is better than betrayal, and sharing better than exploitation."[4]

While almost everyone might agree that leaders should be honest and moral, how do we choose leaders in the first place? Are some simply born to be leaders while others are born to be followers? Leaders do not tumble out of the sky full-blown and credible. Some legitimizing process opens the door to provide leadership for us. In fact, followers often are the key to an effective leader. Someone said, "If you think you are a leader, look behind you. If anyone is following, you are a leader." Some leaders are appointed by others. Some simply emerge—no one else is leading and someone has to. Some are reluctant to take over any kind of leadership, but they will do so if coerced strongly enough by a group. Others love to lead and just automatically take over whenever there is a leadership opportunity.

Regardless of the circumstances under which one becomes a leader, there is no question about the truth of the following statement: *Who you are determines what you do as a leader.* Although many would agree offhandedly with that statement, it is the expressed opinion of James David Barber, one of Duke University's

---

3. Kouzes and Posner, *Leadership Challenge*, 21.
4. Harmin, *Educational Leadership*, 24–30.

political scientists. Barber believes that studying the personalities of American presidents can predict their performance in office. He points out that executives are either "active" or "passive" in their actions as leaders, and they are either "positive" or "negative" in their pursuit of power and their goals. Barber categorizes our past presidents accordingly. He sees both Roosevelts, John Kennedy, and Harry Truman as "active-positives." They were active in their relationships and comfortable with the exercise of their offices. Tragedy-prone presidents, such as Nixon and Lyndon Johnson, are considered "active-negative" because of their negative use of power. Reagan, Harding, and Taft are "passive-positives" in Barber's view because they were not able to exercise initiative toward others easily. Coolidge is one example of a "passive-negative" president.[5]

Barber's point is that our characters will probably predict our leadership styles. We act on what we value. If we are active and positive people, our leadership will reflect active and positive actions. If our standard of morality is high, our leadership will reflect that morality. None of us is a better leader than we are a person. Many people might seem to be better leaders than they are persons. However, think back over the past few years and note how many apparently "wonderful" leaders actually fell into immorality, disgrace, or deceptive practices—all because they pretended to be more moral in the public eye than they really were. Morality is lacking when there is any violation of trust or integrity or when there is any mistreatment of other human beings.

Margaret Thatcher, former prime minister of Great Britain, gave the concluding lecture in a seminar at Hillsdale's Center for Constructive Alternatives. She examined how the Judeo-Christian tradition has provided the moral foundations of America and other nations in the West, and she contrasts the United States' experience with that of the former Soviet Union. She states, "The moral foundations of the American founding history has taught us that freedom cannot long survive unless it is based on moral foundations."[6]

5. Barber, *Presidential Character*, 367–90.
6. Thatcher, *Moral Foundations of Society*, 1.

Moral Leadership in the Founding of America

America's founding years bear witness to that truth, continues Ms. Thatcher. Though the United States has become the most powerful nation, yet she uses her power not for territorial expansion but to perpetuate freedom and justice throughout the world. The United States believes in freedom for all people. Such a belief springs from her spiritual heritage, which began with the founding fathers. John Adams, second president of the United States, wrote, "Our Constitution was designed only for a moral and religious people. It is wholly inadequate for the government of any other."[7]

Former President Calvin Coolidge said that "the foundations of our society and our government rest so much on the teachings of the Bible that it would be difficult to support them if faith in these teachings would cease to be practically universal in our country."[8]

John Winthrop, who led the "Great Migration" to America in the seventeenth century and who helped found the Massachusetts Bay Colony, declared, "We shall be as a City upon a Hill." He told the people that they must "learn to live as God intended men should live: in charity, love, and cooperation with one another.... Most of the early colonists... tried to live in accord with a biblical ethic."[9] It took tremendous courage for American colonists to set out on a dangerous journey to fulfill their faith.

The faith of America's founders affirmed the sanctity of each individual—every human life was equal in the eyes of the Lord God. The Ten Commandments of Moses gave people a sense of obligation toward each other, observes Thatcher.[10] Pre-Christian philosophers such as Plato and Aristotle knew that responsibility was the price of freedom. Sir Edward Gibbon, author of *The Decline and Fall of the Roman Empire,* judged that in the end the Athenians wanted security more than freedom. Yet they lost everything—security, comfort, and freedom—because they wanted not to give to society but for society to give to them. The freedom they were after

---

7. Ibid.
8. Thomas, Speech at Heritage Foundation, 4.
9. Thatcher, *Moral Foundations,* 1.
10. Ibid., 2.

was freedom from responsibility.[11] No wonder they fell. As long as freedom is grounded in responsibility and morality, it will last. Free societies are the only societies with moral foundations, and those foundations are evident in their political, economic, legal, cultural, and most importantly, spiritual lives.[12]

In many areas, Western civilization and the American way of life have risen to the highest standards of honor, justice, morality, and esteem for life. It is obvious that these qualities are the foundation of Western progress—and actually have been the foundation of Western life for hundreds of years. But recently the issue of the value we give to life came along to be tested. The issue is not simply abortion, but the value we give to life.[13] In nature the preservation of life is the most basic and powerful motivation. Consequently, except for a few of the lowest forms of species, family is a primary drive of life. Few creatures in existence will not quickly sacrifice their own lives to protect their young. It is unnatural for a mother to destroy her child, born or unborn; such an action reveals a fundamental departure from civilization and a moving toward barbarism. Joyner believes that there will be no peace of mind on earth until life is esteemed above ambition or convenience.[14] It is not difficult to see that the preservation of life is fundamental to nature and to morality.

Just because something is legal, does not automatically make it moral. Fundamental laws prevail in nature, and these laws reveal that the true nature of morality is doing what is right—regardless of mere legal compliance. A civilization not based on law will degenerate into despotism and tyranny. But a civilization that cannot rise *above* the law to live by what is moral (not just legal) has degenerated already and has lost its potential for true greatness. Just as lawlessness results in tyranny, so will the inability to rise above the law for morality's sake result in tyranny.[15]

---

11. Ibid., 2.
12. Ibid., 5.
13. Joyner, *Leadership, Management*, 57.
14. Ibid., 58.
15. Ibid., 58.

The primary decline in the American family (and in American productivity) is selfishness. Family is primordial. History will verify that the quickest way to destroy a civilization is to destroy the morality that esteems the family.[16] After the family, people in general should be the greatest concern. To see an enterprise or company as a "thing" is to dehumanize the enterprise and the people who comprise it. People are never "things" to control or manipulate. The concept applies to any organization and the people who support that organization as well as to literal family units. The people who comprise the company are more important than the profits or the esteem of the company itself. People are not objects. They are subjects.

"The Founding Fathers' vision was for a constitutional republic where the will of the people would be imposed on Washington [the government], not the views of Washington [the government] imposed on the people." In referring to the intentions of the founding fathers, John Ashcroft quotes Hamilton's famous phrase, "Here, Sir, the people govern." And Ashcroft asks, "Can it still be said that the people govern the United States?"[17] This collective wisdom is evident in that important statement.

For leadership to be successful, it is essential that one delineate the necessary qualities, characteristics, and approaches for leadership of each specific environment. Some people project the future directions of our country and world, specifying which leadership styles may be relevant for future businesses and governments. However, forecasting techniques will always have limits; we still cannot be certain what the future will bring. World-renowned thinker, Decrane, however, suggests that there is one model that can help us put some meaningful concepts into leadership in business. He calls it the "constitutional model" because James Madison and other framers of the U. S. Constitution "constructed a document embodying certain core principles to guide the lives of the American people and to establish the framework of governance."[18]

16. Ibid., 59.
17. Ashcroft, *Moral Leadership in Politics*, 1–4.
18. Decrane, *Leaders of the Future*, 250.

Moral Leadership

These framers constructed a document that had to be worded broadly enough to be effective for many specific daily issues as well as for changing conditions and for future challenges they could not even envision. Even so, many years later, in the twenty-first century, we still see that the fundamental principles guiding the Constitution continue to survive, regardless of the huge number of amendments and attempts to interpret them in ways amenable to specific purposes.

In the same way, we can identify core qualities of leadership, even though they may need to be qualified, modified, and reapplied as conditions change and new challenges arise. The truly basic qualities remain solid and relevant.[19] Those core qualities of leadership would include, in addition to basic leadership skills, character, vision, behavior, and confidence. These traits endure despite all social, political, cultural, and business changes. These basic leadership principles help individuals at all stages of responsibility to lead and to model what a leader should be. The constitutional model suggests that leaders will adapt these core competencies to the challenges of their time and the areas of their responsibilities.

Community occurs when free people with some sense of equal worth join together voluntarily for a common goal. This is most easily done in small organizations affording face-to-face contact. Larger organizations find it difficult to create enough personal contact and common vision to guide actions down the hierarchy of leadership. The larger and more complex the organization or group, the more difficult it is to reach a common vision and to derive enough community spirit to guide actions without also increasing the chain of command. The larger the chain of command, the more likely will the sense of community become undone. As the power of community spirit is stretched thin, the chain of command fills the void, and the sense of community declines further.[20]

The organizations that first hit the wall of complexity and thus were in need of institutions to distribute leadership were the largest organizations of all—whole societies and nations. Leaders of

---

19. Ibid.
20. Pinchot, *Leaders of the Future, New Vision*, 28.

successful nations, then, have become the models of good leadership techniques. Centuries ago, nations began reaching the limits of direct leadership. The diversity of tasks was simply too great for any one king or dictator to run everything effectively.[21] Western European nations gave the free market a major role in their economy. The nations in the Warsaw Pact, that ran their economies with centrally controlled ministries, fell behind in wealth and human contentment. China, by freeing her nation's entrepreneurial spirit from the Communist Party, has allowed its leaders to achieve double-digit economic growth. South Korea, Chile, Singapore, Peru, and Taiwan have all achieved economic growth after freeing their markets. Could the same level of growth in productivity and innovation become available to leaders of corporations? The more freedom allowed, the more indirect the leadership. Since direct leadership has imposed limitations, the largest groups, especially nations, must move into free enterprise and indirect leadership.

As the complexity of an organization reaches beyond direct leadership, the leader's main purpose is contributing to the corporate culture and the corporate institutions that make freedom work and that create a freer society within the organization.[22] The freer society will be based on values such as respect for all people, freedom of choice, speech, and assembly, as well as fairness and justice. The leadership, at this point, will be the best kind of government of a free nation. Such leaders will bring out the best in others and will listen to their followers.

Our founding fathers knew the day would come when "liberty would hang in a balance. . . . They believed that liberty could not survive without morality. Our liberties are in danger because Americans have become an immoral people."[23] This statement is verified by the fact that a majority of Americans say that character isn't important in political leaders. Calvin Coolidge, however, showed a great deal of insight when he stated, "If we are to maintain the great heritage which has been bequeathed to us, we must

---

21. Ibid., 29.
22. Ibid., 38.
23. Mostert, ed., *What True Americanism Demands*, note 1.

Moral Leadership

be like-minded as the fathers who created it. . . . . We must follow the spiritual and moral leadership which they showed." Coolidge pointed out that the foundations of our country were not material, but spiritual and moral: "No other theory is adequate to explain or comprehend the Declaration of Independence . . . it is the product of the spiritual insight of the people." And Coolidge concludes by asserting, "Unless the faith of the American people . . . is to endure, the principles of our Declaration will perish."[24]

Consequently, though many today may say that character is not important in leaders, we have much evidence that character and morality are indeed as important in leadership as they are in other areas of our American way of life. In fact, a big advertisement in the *Wall Street Journal* announcing a new book by Bill George for corporate leaders led out with this large heading: "Character still counts!"[25] And it definitely has counted for years. Calvin Coolidge stated, "We do not need more intellectual power, we need more moral power. We do not need more knowledge, we need more character.[26]" His statement is still true today.

---

24. Thomas, Speech at Heritage Foundation, 5.
25. George, "Authentic Leadership," *Wall Street Journal*, 2003.
26. Thomas, Speech at Heritage Foundation, 1996.

two

The Ten Commandments as the Roots of American Culture

THE DECLARATION OF INDEPENDENCE and the Gettysburg Address are two of the most famous and widely circulated vision statements ever composed. Together they are the spiritual constitution of the United States, and each served a great purpose when they were written. Both documents, poetic enough to be literature, mingle the controversy of the time with the broad outlook of a noble appeal for the dignity and rights of Americans. And both are reasoned enough to carry conviction yet inspire enthusiasm among followers. They are empowering statements that have impacted our nation for many years. They have established a system of ethics and morality to govern our nation.

Moral Leadership has always had a place in our country. We may not see it for periods of time as we look around and think that all leadership around us is corrupt. However, there has always been a remnant of leaders with strong moral codes of behavior who have stood their ground for the right way of dealing with fellow human beings. Some of those moral leaders have been national or state leaders—presidents, congressmen, senators, state officers, and city leaders. Others have been leaders in less lofty areas—church deacons, managers of work places, clerks at community offices, and

Moral Leadership

privates in the army. But whether in a large pool or a small pool, these leaders have reminded us that morality exists and that it is important to keep our own moral code in good repair, to behave to others as we would like them to behave to us.

Many organizational leaders believe it is possible to violate ethical and moral standards of action and still profit from their business and their clientele. However, such actions usually end up hurting the businesses and alienating the employees or followers. It all comes down to right and wrong. Leaders cannot continue to violate the right and wrong of the society in which they work if they want to continue to gain in their businesses. As Bob Allen, AT&T executive, said, "You can't win out in the long run by . . . taking short-run advantage that is ethically or morally wrong. You err on the side of being absolutely pure. I do business with almost anybody as long as they are willing to negotiate on moral and ethical terms."[1]

How does this kind of moral integrity relate to, or connect to, leadership in general in the United States? The recent debate over the legitimacy of hanging copies of the Ten Commandments in schoolrooms and courtrooms illustrates the problem in our nation with moral living and moral leadership. The Ten Commandments from the Bible were originally accepted as the basis for the founding of our nation. Our Founding Fathers referred to them and used them as a basis for the moral essentials of our country. In fact, James Madison, the father of the Constitution, said, "We have staked the entire future of the American civilization not upon the power of government but upon the capacity of the individual to govern himself, control himself, and sustain himself according to the Ten Commandments of God."

Many people believe the Ten Commandments have no place in our public lives—certainly not in schools and courts. They believe, suddenly and only recently, that putting the Ten Commandments on the wall in a classroom or courtroom in the United States is a radical, dangerous attempt to overthrow our American freedoms. In fact, some are incensed that the "Christians" in

---

1. Haas, *Leader Within*, 157.

The Ten Commandments as the Roots of American Culture

this country are trying to take over the founding documents by claiming biblical references and heritage as if such does not exist. However, a look at the original documents of our founding Fathers will prove without a doubt that the founding Fathers deliberately worked from the premise of the morality of the Holy Bible, especially from the Ten Commandments. Many seem to have forgotten that George Washington, in his farewell address as leader of the United States of America, said, "It is impossible to govern this country or any country in the world rightly without a belief in God and the Ten Commandments."

Because some people today are not familiar with the Ten Commandments (aside from hearing the controversy about them in the newspapers), perhaps a short review of what they are and what they intend to do would be helpful.

The Ten Commandments as given in Exodus 20 can be abbreviated to these:

1. You shall have no god before Me (the Judeo-Christian Lord God).
2. You shall not make idols in any form or worship idols in any form.
3. You shall not misuse the name of the Lord (in swearing and prophesying).
4. You shall keep the Sabbath day holy.
5. You shall honor your father and mother.
6. You shall not murder.
7. You shall not commit adultery.
8. You shall not steal.
9. You shall not lie (or give any kind of false testimony).
10. You shall not covet anything that belongs to anyone else.

These ten "commands" are statements of the way to act if we would be moral people. Notice that only the first and third commandments have anything directly to say about God, although the second commandment could be implied to do so as well. People mistakenly think that the Ten Commandments are all about religion or worshipping God. Not so.

They are about living a decent moral life in community with other people. They are about being human and treating others as human beings too. They have to do with every person's relationship to every other person. We cannot violate these standards of behavior in our relationships to those around us and still call ourselves moral beings or even human beings at all as we were intended to be. This is common good behavior—for leaders as well as for followers.

It is interesting to note that one can attempt to keep all of the Ten Commandments with no outside help—religious or otherwise. It is certainly possible for all of us, if we use our best judgment and discipline, to try to obey all of these on our own—by our own ability (though we will always fail at some point). In other words, human beings are not amoral creatures as are animals. We are all capable of displaying morality. We do not always choose to act accordingly, however. It is much easier to lie sometimes than to be the moral person who tells the truth. Our society often excuses an addict for his drug habit, giving him the benefit of the doubt and assuming he is not able to help himself. But that same society has different standards when it comes to lying, cheating, and living in any other immoral way. Society wants to blame our moral failures on our inability to keep such stringent demands from a stern God. However, notice that God asks nothing of us that we are not able to do ourselves.

We live in community with other human beings, and God knows that for the community to survive, certain rules or laws must be in effect. These ten "rules" (or "commands" for living in community) that God has given are the basic core of survival. Without them, the community is destroyed.

However, there is another way of looking at these commandments. In the New Testament, the part of the Bible that tells of Christianity and life after Jesus came to earth, we are told how to transfer the commandments of action given in the Old Testament

The Ten Commandments as the Roots of American Culture

(the ten things we must do to survive in community) to commandments of attitude. Moral beings live by attitude more than by actions. How easy it is for actions to measure up to some sort of code of behavior while the mind and heart are bitter, resentful, angry, hateful, and feeling just the opposite of what the bodily actions indicate. In other words, we can politely say, "I'm sorry," when our parents or teachers coerce us to do something, while at the same time hatefully saying in our hearts, "I'm glad I kicked your face in."

There may often be a huge discrepancy between action and attitude. Jesus deals with this discrepancy in His teachings on the Ten Commandments. In the book of Matthew, Jesus refocuses the commandment from the *action* of murder to the *attitude* of murder by telling us that murder is not just the action of killing someone, but it is the attitude of being really angry with our brothers and neighbors.[2] He tells us that adultery is not simply taking someone who is not our spouse (an action), but it is looking at someone lustfully (an attitude) whether we take that person or not: "But I say to you that whoever looks on a woman to lust after her has committed adultery with her already in his heart."[3]

Moral living, then, is based not simply on the physical keeping of the law or of the Ten Commandments of the Old Testament, but it is keeping the intent of the law in our hearts and minds. It is being willing to live according to the moral context behind the laws rather than trying to get around or avoid their meaning. If we want to live morally pure lives, we must keep our bodies and minds in control. The Ten Commandments requires this of us, whether we are speaking of actions or attitudes. Living in community requires that we follow basic commands of getting along with others and valuing the lives of others.

Why, then, is it so difficult for people to abide by the Ten Commandments? Most of us would agree that we do not want others to lie, cheat, murder, commit adultery with our spouses, or covet our possessions. Why then, will we not keep the commands ourselves if we want others to do so? The basic problem

---

2. Matt. 5: 21–26, MEV.
3. Matt. 5:28, MEV.

is Commandment One. If we truly love the Lord God first—put no other gods or possessions or people before Him—then we can keep the rest of the commands with little trouble. But most people like to put themselves first, or put their careers, possessions, fame, or health first. Those things or people who are most important to us are the ones who become our "gods" or "idols" (as mentioned in Command Two). Because we do not acknowledge God first, we have no reason to follow the rest of the commands—there is no longer any social, physical, political, or economic reason to keep the Ten Commandments. No one will pay us to keep them. The only reason for keeping them is the moral one. And if it suits us to lie or violate any of the other nine commands, we do so. Once we break one command, it is very easy to break all the rest of them. We may not actually kill a person, but we will allow ourselves to hate someone to the extent that we almost wish that person dead— the same as committing murder.

Because our government (national, state, and local) has not kept the code of morality alive in their dealings with the American people, many people of our nation, in turn, do not keep moral conduct toward the government. Our leaders break the Ten Commandments every day in the political life, the social life, and the physical life of our nation. No wonder they do not want the Ten Commandments on the walls of our courts and public buildings— the reminder of those standards brings too much guilt and shame on the actions taking place in those buildings. The people of our nation know the leaders lie and cheat, so the people see no reason they should not follow suit. If the big leaders get away with it, why shouldn't the small everyday people also get away with it? So the moral code goes out with the garbage and the morality of the nation degenerates to selfishness and trying to get away with more than the other guy gets away with.

How, then, does this moral stance of a nation relate to the morality of leadership? The concepts in the Ten Commandments apply to all phases of life and all areas of relationships. A successful leader will not continue to be successful if he or she begins to lie, steal, cheat, or murder those who get in the way of success.

The Ten Commandments as the Roots of American Culture

Although our country's moral position is not what it used to be in the early days of our founding, we do not individually want to follow a leader who is known to be dishonest and undependable. So whether or not a leader claims any religious affiliation, we want that leader to live according to the rules of living in community. We want that leader to be trustworthy and dependable. As we look in later chapters at the most desired traits of a leader, we will notice that many of those traits have to do with the moral character of that leader rather than with his economic or social stance or abilities. The realm of moral character, therefore, remains closely associated with the Ten Commandments.

Perhaps the most important connection between the Ten Commandments and leadership is simply that the commandments deal with relationships between people. Robert D. Dale, in his book on leadership, creates the ten commandments of leaders. His commandments are aimed primarily at the leadership of teams, but they are applicable to all leaders as well, because he considers the leader in relationship to the people he leads. Though Dale labels his list as "commandments," he also calls them ten principles to follow in team building. The first five focus on concerns with people, and the second five focus on production issues. These two parts of leadership must be maintained in balance—people as well as production. Here are Dale's commandments:

1. Develop personal ownership of your team's life and work. People support what they help create.

2. Surface expectations. Everyone expects something from the groups he or she is involved with. Recognize there are different personal agendas and work together.

3. Create a "we" climate. A "we" climate comes when leaders take responsibility for failures and share the successes.

4. Recognize relational roles in teams. A broad range of relational roles will exist in any group.

5. Do team repair. Groups need maintenance to run smoothly.

6. Define the core mission of your organization. No team can function productively without a clear vision of its task.
7. Identify the formal task groups you work with. There may be an overlap of members' responsibilities. Note the overlapping members and be aware of when to change hats. Select the right hat for each occasion.
8. Develop team task descriptions. Efficient job descriptions cut down on gaps and overlaps.
9. Monitor task roles on the team. Having some who can fill several roles aids the whole team.
10. Learn to manage meetings. Guiding a process in meetings is better than controlling people.[4]

Any organization is made up of a wide variety of teams. Some teams work together better than others. The goal of a leader is to put together all the diverse gifts, roles, and resources of a group of people and have them function for a common cause. When this is done, the leader has succeeded.

In a kind of parallel to the idea of the Ten Commandments, authors James Kouzes and Barry Posner, have coined what they call the "Ten Commitments of Leadership." These ten commitments are sub headings under their five fundamental practices of exemplary leadership and serve as the basis for learning to lead. Their five fundamental practices of exemplary leadership are these: Challenging the process, inspiring a shared vision, enabling others to act, modeling the way, and encouraging the heart. The Ten Commitments, then, which are sub-points of those five, are as follows:

1. Search out challenging opportunities to change, grow, innovate, and improve.
2. Experiment, take risks, and learn from the accompanying mistakes.
3. Envision an uplifting and ennobling future.

4. Dale, *Ministers as Leaders*, 100–104.

4. Enlist others in a common vision by appealing to their values, interests, hopes, and dreams.
5. Foster collaboration by promoting cooperative goals and building trust.
6. Strengthen people by giving power away, providing choice, developing competence, assigning critical tasks, and offering visible support.
7. Set the example by behaving in ways that are consistent with shared values.
8. Achieve small wins that promote consistent progress and build commitment.
9. Recognize individual contributions to the success of every project.
10. Celebrate team accomplishments regularly.[5]

Notice that in both lists—whether commitments or commandments—the key focus is on the people involved. If a leader ignores the people who are following, then that leader might as well count on not being a successful leader. Moral leadership demands that a leader put the welfare of people first.

The key factor, then, in effective leadership is morality and moral values. The degree to which leaders adhere to moral values is the degree to which they will be successful. The ambiguity in the phrase "moral values" must be clarified. Morality and moral values are not religious in nature. Many religions use morality as an important part of their belief systems, but the term itself, and the conduct depicting morality, is not religious. A closer tie would be ethics.

Even "spiritual values" are not necessarily religious, for "spiritual" is most often contrasted with material, physical or corporeal (rather than with God or religion). In fact, *The Oxford Dictionary* defines *spiritual* as "of spirit as opposed to matter." It defines *spirit* as the "intelligent or immaterial part of man, soul." These

---

5. Kouzes and Posner, *Leadership Challenge*, 17–18.

definitions suggest the dual nature of humankind—spiritual and material. A human being functions through the physical body and also through the intellect and will. These uses of the terms are common—attempting to separate tangible or physical activity and standards with those not physical. Morality, then, often associated with the spiritual part of man rather than the physical, refers to actions that might be seen in any human being in any country and of any religious belief whatsoever.

Therefore, even though moral standards might vary in different cultures, some basic tenets are similar. For instance, it is usually considered wrong to steal from another in any culture—thus stealing is an immoral act that a moral person would not do. This is a philosophical or secular value—not religious. For this reason Rick Garlikov, in his article "Moral and Spiritual Values," can qualify that "Moral laws are general, sometimes abstract, principles about how things ought to be," . . . discovered through our "collective moral sensitivity, understanding, judgment, and wisdom.[6]" Moral ideas, then, are right or wrong depending on their content—what they say, rather than on who said them.

Moral reasoning leads us to apply the principles of morality to any situation or issue at any time. Leadership is no exception. And perhaps it is even more important to use all the moral sense we have when we lead, even more so than at any other time, because our followers are watching and learning from us.

In the next chapter, we will consider some specifics of moral leadership.

---

6. Garlikov, "Moral and Spiritual Values," 3.

three

The Nine Leadership Traits

OF THE DOZENS, EVEN hundreds, of books on leadership, most will offer a list of seven, eight, nine, or ten attributes or desirable traits of a good leader, calling these traits essential to good leadership. Many of the attributes thus presented as leadership traits are really platitudes of expectation or action and so become simply intriguing things to do—actions on the surface level only. Those traits seldom have anything to do with developing the heart, mind, or soul of a leader—where real people reside. But the following Nine Leadership Traits reveal character, reflecting the person a moral leader *can be*, as distinct from what a moral leader *can do*.

The concept of character has been severely watered down by many facets of the media and educational institutions that are responsible for producing today's leaders. Most institutions teach that all people have character regardless of whom they might be or how they might live. This philosophy is relativism. Relativism is the belief that there are no moral absolutes. There are many underlying premises of relativism. The basic premise is that humankind is inherently good. If that premise were true, it would follow that everyone has character. Another underlying premise of relativism is that there is no normative value system distinguishing right from wrong. In other words, right and wrong are relative to each individual.

If there are no moral absolutes, relativists must necessarily propound a distorted meaning of character. They cannot define a specific view of character since everything is relative to them. If character means anything in a moral sense at all, its definition cannot fluctuate. One might wonder how relativists could define anything if nothing is absolute. However, whatever character means, they believe they have it. At best, it appears that what they really have going for them would be simply good habits. But all of us know that even animals learn good habits. One should note that animals are amoral. Consequently, this level of existence is the level to which relativism reduces its adherents. But good habits are not useless, for good habits can accentuate character. Though people are not born with habits, most of which can be formed or broken within thirty days. People are born with the instinct to develop character, and they do develop it over time unless they lose it through immoral choices. However, character is not automatically positive, and must be developed into positive arenas throughout one's life. Character, in fact, requires a lifetime to refine, as does leadership.

Although those who believe in relativism may have to admit that certain people are devoid of character from a moral standpoint, people of character must accept relativists unconditionally without expecting them to be something other than what they are. Helping people feel accepted the way they are has the propensity to enhance their vision of what they can become. Such is the only way we can free them from the limitations of relativism so that they can truly change and become people of character.

These leadership traits are steeped in an age-old tradition of character, and we should expect to see them in any moral leader. A true leader leads with spirit as well as with physical presence.

The Nine Leadership Traits define the mature moral leader. A true leader is a person whose life and character conform to ethical and moral standards of human integrity. Patterning one's life after moral guidelines is not a "religious" thing to do. It is instead

The Nine Leadership Traits

recognition of the value of those areas of character that are usually developed through giving attention to the non-physical, or moral, part of man. Such attention alters a person's life-style because the character is then developed through higher values, moral channels, rather than through the physical or fleshly means of using people or of trying to satisfy our desire for money and possessions. Such traits of leadership are especially important in relationships between leaders and followers.

The traits of those who follow a moral lifestyle can be contrasted to the purely physical actions in those who do not choose to live morally. Physical actions include traits such as sexual immorality, impurity, debauchery, hatred, discord, jealousy, rage, selfish ambition, envy, drunkenness, lying, or any kind of immoral act or thought. The physical nature of man produces actions, thoughts, and desires that are self-seeking and base. These are the traits we should never expect to find in a moral leader. Moral leaders, then, can be identified both by how they act and how they do not act.

The Nine Traits of an effective moral leader would identify a person of acuity, indeed a balanced leader. These traits do not come naturally, as an integral part of a human's own nature. One is not born with them. They come directly from the effort of moving out of the position of one's own nature—the reality of what is, and moving into the nature of what should be. Such growth does not depend upon natural circumstances but is the result of the leader's hard work to become the best possible leader.

Neither do these Nine Traits come from self-imposed discipline. One can be highly moral and not have these traits, but one cannot have these traits and not be highly moral. Such character is the natural outcome, by a process of steady growth, of a principle of life *within*. The Nine Traits are not divided up between leaders. Honesty is not given to one person and power to another. These traits have to do with character—what a person is—and a truly moral person should exhibit all of them. Their effectiveness comes as they work together within a leader.

Disciplining the self to allow the character traits to develop will yield results. Remember what Abraham Lincoln said, "Always bear in mind that your own resolution to success is more important than any other one thing." The traits will come as leaders begin to separate themselves from the wrong types of goals, yield themselves to the values and character of moral discipline, and seek to know and practice the kind of leadership that seeks the good of all. Thus leaders yield their own natural desires to the moral teachings of selflessness.

Here are the Nine Leadership Traits.

1. INDIVIDUALITY

Rising above group thought, taking a risk by going against the majority's opinion, doing something different, even if it means establishing a new precedent—these are traits showing individuality. John F. Kennedy, previous president of the United States, once said, "Unity of freedom has never relied on uniformity of opinion."

How would you like to go to work every day for a company that said, "Welcome, we're just like everyone else"? Uniqueness brings a sense of pride. There must be something to differentiate us from others if we want to attract business, employees, clients, donors, investors, or even volunteers. The prouder we are of the organization/group we are part of, the more loyal we will be to that group. Smaller divisions/departments of the whole organization can also demonstrate some traits of individuality or distinctive purpose, in order to distinguish them from other parts of the whole. Smaller units, within the group (of a city, neighborhood, corporation, public agency, school, religious institution, etc.) can find their unique image as they work for the common future of the larger organization.

Leaders with a desire to be individualistic will need to find a way to personalize the group's activity or product so that not only the customer but also the employees and associates as well will not be depersonalized. With a personal approach to people, a leader will find ways to keep the company from being just like everyone else.

The Nine Leadership Traits

An individualistic leader is not the same as an independent leader. Independent leaders tend to work on their own, ignoring the need for team unity and shared vision. Individual leaders, on the other hand, are those who dare to be themselves rather than one more rubber-stamped company head. Independent leaders tend to be competitive. And though there are times when competition counts, it is not usually a good leadership trait. Dean and Mary Tjosvold conducted a study that showed that leaders with cooperative relationships inspired more commitment and were considered more competent than were competitive and independent leaders. Competitive leaders were seen as obstructive and ineffective.[1]

Robert D. Hof stated that "Innovation has to be a twenty-four-hour-a-day job." He indicates that individuality is not always the more comfortable method of leadership, and he agrees with Amazon Chief Executive Jeff Bezos who told a group of Stanford University students last year, "Invention always leads you down paths that people think are weird." Hof suggests the futility of a competitive conflict between leaders, but he does push for individualism in leadership. He states, "Don't just get bigger, get unique."[2]

Harvard Business School strategy guru Michael E. Porter agrees. He says, "There is no best auto company, there is no best car. "You're really competing to be unique." It is this attempt to be unique that puts leaders in the position of being individuals—not just another one of the pack. For example the leaders of Whole Foods Market are not trying to compete with supermarkets but are trying to meet the needs of a certain group of customers. Caterpillar is number one in heavy equipment, but the leaders of Caterpillar do not take that position for granted. The company has a goal to keep in mind: What its customers want. Because the company offers customer service second to none, its customers are loyal. The leaders of the company were individualistic enough to commit to a risky plan—offer service anywhere in the world. Others

---

1. Tjosvoid, *Leading the Team Organization*, 34.
2. Hof, "How to Hit a Moving Target," 77, 81–82.

afraid of taking a risk wouldn't have profited from such a dramatic rise in profits.³

Individualistic leaders are not afraid to get personal with their followers and clients. We have seen companies merging so quickly these days that our market place has become a mass-market with huge chains such as Wal-Mart, Microsoft, Home Depot, Macy's, as well as huge insurance and financial corporations. Gone are the possible profits for individually owned corner markets. For example, Amazon.com has an amazing "18,038 business books listed that mention the word "competitiveness."⁴

One of the dangers of being individualistic is that such a leader tends to foster strong personal dependencies from some followers. People who are not very creative themselves often attach themselves to those who are creative; they enjoy being part of the process. However, such people cannot easily break free of strong dependencies. Innovative programs tend to be associated with the leaders who establish them. Leaders need to be aware of possible dependencies and help members to draw their resources from a number of sources, including one another. Mutual support from other followers is healthful teamwork.

Innovation requires a willingness to look at change as an opportunity. Innovation doesn't necessarily create change, but most innovation is to improve (and thus bring a change to) the market, product, internal efficiency, the employee, or so on. Thus innovation by nature seems to look for opportunities that change might offer. Innovative leadership is important because our society is changing so quickly with such frequent (it seems almost daily) technological advances. Our society is not only knowledge-based, but it is wired to bring advances never before even thought of.

Peter Drucker reports, "In a crafts society, which ours essentially was until late in the nineteenth century, major changes occurred perhaps every eighty years. In military technology, between the disappearance of the longbow in the reign of Elizabeth I and the launching of the *Dreadnought*, the first of a class of British

---

3. Ibid., 82.
4. Ibid., 83.

battleships, in 1906, a significant innovation took place every sixty years. Today, courtesy of the Pentagon, it is probably every sixty days."[5]

Drucker has made a good guess for the 1990s, but now in the twenty-first century the rate of change in computer technology alone is measured in hours and days rather than months. But Drucker is right when he adds that "the center of gravity of knowledge is constantly on the move."[6] Consequently, any leader who is not innovative will certainly be left behind in any market. Innovation means change because it means leaving the old and trying something new. To get at something better, we have to be willing to throw out (or revise) the old and comfortable as well as the mistakes and unproductive practices of the past.

Organizational change can be very costly to some people. As organizations change, it is important to notice what is happening to those caught up in the process. Leaders need to be aware of the interests of weaker and quieter people because these tend not to advocate for themselves. The same change may benefit some and hurt others. Good communication and prompt action to ameliorate conflict will develop cooperation and a feeling of commitment from all involved.

The most crucial time of an organizational change is the first few months. After a program has been established, when a group is changing its direction, there are multiple reasons and opportunities for conflict. A leader must begin well when offering change. Impressions made, habits established, attitudes encouraged, and structures developed will probably determine the shape of the organization for years to come. How a leader begins that change is crucial. Leaders must be sure that everyone is included and understands the part to be played. Good communication within and among the group conveys accurate information and gives opportunity to correct misinformation. It provides open channels from leaders to membership/followers. It is as necessary to the healthy

---

5. Drucker, *Managing for the Future*, 339.
6. Ibid.

function of an organization as the circulatory system is to a healthy human body.

Knowledge and skill depreciate, so effective leaders must be involved in the continuous process of lifelong learning. Individuals never stop learning. Learning is essential to both personal and organization vitality. Often, people who want to be leaders must first spend time discovering who they are. Self-development is part of the learning necessary to grow professionally. Self-confidence is really the ability to believe in one's own powers. Individualistic leaders must understand how the organization operates, what kind of problems they will need to solve, what their own strengths and weaknesses are, and how they can move the organization along to further growth. Such knowledge is never static but moves and morphs with changing times. Thus, the lifelong learning process is partially self-learning; however, it is also learning about emerging markets, changing social mores, new economic trends, or whatever areas are applicable to the group/company as a whole.

The individualists, as life-long learners, must be open to changing global views. Thus they must learn as much as possible about the forces that will affect the group—whether those are political, economic, social, moral, artistic, or other forces. Such learners must also continue to improve their understanding of their co-workers and followers. Leaders must be interpersonally competent, able to listen, take advice, and develop the trust of others.

There is a danger of being too innovative, or too pushy with innovation. Leaders must be constantly aware that they are working with a group, with other individuals. Challenging the status quo simply to promote innovation can be destructive and create dissension. Pushing leaders' own inspiration at the expense of others involved can cause others to give up and not even try. Learning about and being aware of co-workers, and their strengths and weaknesses, will help solve this potential problem.

John Gardner, Stanford professor and former secretary of Health, Education, and Welfare, writes that there are four moral goals of leadership:

The Nine Leadership Traits

1. Releasing human potential
2. Balancing the needs of individuals and the company
3. Defending the fundamental values of the community
4. Instilling in individuals a sense of initiative and responsibility[7]

Leaders who are especially innovative are usually good at number four—inspiring others to be innovative too. However, we should also notice the second half of number four; innovation and innovative thinking has a dimension of responsibility that must not be ignored. And there are also the first three goals to remember—none of the goals works in a vacuum. Those who think and act in unusual or imaginative ways have the responsibility to communicate and educate those followers and co-workers who will support those individualistic and innovative ideas.

Individualistic leaders must also exercise a great deal of self-control because, especially for the one who is always in control of the group or team, it is easy to assume one always knows best. Self-control, temperance, moderation, and self-restraint are all terms used to define the ability to control one's own actions and speech. The concept of self-control covers the whole range of human appetites, implying not only control over the physical self, but also over the mental and emotional. The power to be temperate in all things is an important virtue and a mark of growth. The necessary self-control cannot be attained by natural self-discipline. The possibilities are just as great for those with minimal personal strength of character as for those with strong wills of their own.

The demands for physical self-control are fairly obvious to most of us. However, often we overlook the need for emotional or mental self-control or temperance. For example, anger is a common form of intemperance of the emotional life, and it shows itself in many forms. Sulking day after day is as intemperate as a violent outburst. Allowing the tongue to run away with us is a form of intemperance, regardless of whether it is uncontrolled levity, gossip, or abuse of confidences. Inordinate love of praise is intemperate

---

7. Gardner, *Leadership Papers*, 10–18.

and shows a lack of self-control and an unwillingness to give glory to others. Such an attitude focuses attention on the leader alone rather than on the team or group as a whole.

The Greek origin for self-control or moderation suggests the meaning of "to have inward strength." Our inward strength of will must become greater than all the outward strength of temptation, desire, excitement, or peer pressure. This inner strength gives perfect self-control. Most of all, we must remember that a continuous attempt at self-control will strengthen the weakest of us so that others will begin to see in us something of the self-control that all aspire to. The inward strength does not come automatically—it comes from a constant attention to the need for controlling ourselves.

Self-control is not being a stoic. It is not being a stern, rigid, strong-willed cynic. Neither is it a case of "grin and bear it." Self-control is not simply severe self-discipline. Most of us can do some of this some of the time. There are days when we behave in exemplary and commendable ways. However, there are other days when we behave in less than commendable ways—in ways we wish we could later erase. On the days of non-commendable behavior we are out of control, living our own strong-willed lives. Because of this inconsistency, we need to build the strength that comes from practicing self-control.

Self-control for the leader means that the "self" (the whole person, the whole being—body, soul, spirit) comes under control. It means that leaders are individuals governed so that they are able to be an example to those who are following. A leader's entire life, every aspect of it (whether emotional, moral, or physical), has become subject to the needs of the organization and the people comprising that organization. The leader is also a person under authority—the authority of the organization as a whole—just as the followers are under the authority of the leader.

If we want to see this kind of control, we should not simply look to pattern ourselves after the example of other human beings. Even the best of them have faults and make mistakes. We need to focus on our own individual strengths and character, building ourselves to the place where we experience our own growth, maturity, and strength to practice self-control.

Some leaders, indeed almost all people, think that they must exercise a strenuous self-discipline so that the moral attributes can be seen in their lives. When they are criticized, they tell themselves, "Now I must show patience and endurance. I must not lose my temper." But all the time they are ready to explode. Self-discipline alone cannot produce true character because it belongs to self; it is exerting self-will over the negative traits that want to be demonstrated. While such self-exertion will help us to act in better ways towards our followers, what brings a true change of character, or a positive growth in character, is the internalization of the characteristics necessary to develop our own characters. In developing our own characters, we also find the key to leading others to develop their characters.

Control needs to come from inside a leader, not depend on external circumstances or conditions. Anything that makes us lose control is, in effect, conquering us. Since leaders need to be the conquerors, it is up to them to maintain control. We tend to judge ourselves by our intentions, but others judge us by our reactions. Controlling our anger or disagreement requires us to find positive ways to express our feelings. Control will bring a sense of calm to an otherwise potentially explosive situation. Control will allow leaders to listen to others, consider all options, and make the best decision for the organization as a whole.

Individualists tend to listen to opinions of others, but not to be particularly influenced by the last person talked to. They will take independent stands for creative problem solving. Leaders with initiative will seize opportunities of all kinds. They will achieve results through new means—new methods of problem solving. Creativity and initiative help leaders approach a problem again and again—not just once or twice, but in new ways with a different perspective—to come up with a solution. However, leaders do not need to do all the innovative thinking; a good team of followers will brainstorm with the leader to come up with possible solutions.

Individualists do not wait for corporate heads to come along and "fix" whatever needs to be done to improve production or profits. Innovative leaders will evaluate and make their own lists of developmental needs. They will build on their own strengths and overcome their own weaknesses as leaders. Career success will depend on leaders' abilities to be self-reliant, be team players, and be able to function in the middle of corporate or group differences.

So many major corporations seem trapped in a morass of laws, procedures, expectations, rules, and attempts not to violate any status quo. Playing it safe seems to be the first rule of all. A leader, though, must do more than preserve the environment. Many leaders simply learn to play the game—do what is expected, say the right thing, go along with the crowd. A company or group who wishes to grow, however, needs a leader willing to make waves and be innovative. It is important that leaders do play by the rules and that they go through proper channels of the company/group structure. But they do not have to *think* by the rules. In fact the primary quality of individualists is that they think outside the box of rules. Such leaders will not confine their imaginations to what has been done and what has worked in the past. Such thinking leads to mediocrity. The innovative, imaginative individualist comes up with new solutions to old problems.

2. INTEGRITY

Ethics, integrity, morality—these are closely aligned terms all indicating a trait crucial to a leader's character.

Morality includes honesty, along with integrity and ethical actions. To be honest is to be totally trustworthy. If leaders are serious about their relationships with those they lead, they must perform the difficult task of being honest with others—even with difficult people. Honesty is the means by which people expand their sphere of influence, and it begins at home. Without honesty, there is no character. And without character, there is no effective leadership.

When a person is honest, others can see it and sense it. Eventually, the honesty and integrity of one person may influence others to be more honest; however, even if there is no apparent transfer of the trait, a leader must exhibit honesty at all times. People want their leaders to be honest, because they want to follow leaders they can trust, leaders who accept them, leaders who are more concerned with people than with progress or profits. Likewise, honesty empowers leaders to develop relationships with those who would follow them. When honesty and love reach people, truth also reaches them.

Honesty is not emotion or warm feelings or tolerance; neither is it overlooking faults in others. Honesty is a deliberate act of the will, motivated by the welfare of the recipient; it is also motivated by the need to be free from any sham that dishonesty would require. Someone has said honesty is like an orange—it is singular but has various manifestations just as the one orange has several sections. If that is an accurate comparison, the whole fruit would be the trait of honesty and the sections would be integrity, relationships, self-respect, and so forth—all the results of an honest life.

There are many obstacles to absolute honesty. Some people push the edges of honesty to preserve their own self-image; others need to try to make themselves look better to their followers. Sometimes both leaders and followers stand to lose money, a promotion, respect, or image if they are fully honest. We are deluded if we think we can develop an honest approach to our lives and work without putting forth some effort and time for development. The key to honesty is selflessness. Honesty is self-giving, self-sharing, and self-sacrificing because it becomes more important to be honest and act with integrity before our followers than it is to look good in their eyes. Honesty is a powerful life principle. Leaders who are honest are models and examples for all who follow them.

Most people will follow a leader they believe in—a leader who is moral and has integrity. After capability, a leader's moral integrity may inspire more trust and confidence than any other single trait. There can be no leader-follower relationship if there is no trust, and there can be no trust when the leader is not honest enough to be trustworthy. When we follow someone—whether into the boardroom or into battle, into the classroom or into the front office—we must assure ourselves that that person is being truthful, ethical, and principled in thought and action—in other words, worthy of our trust and worthy of being followed. In a survey taken by Kouzes and Posner, they discovered that nearly 90 percent of constituents want their leaders to be honest above all else. The survey also asked how constituents might measure something as subjective as honesty. Respondents indicated that a leader's behavior provided the evidence. In fact, regardless of what leaders said about their own integrity, people observed the behavior and noted the consistency between the words and the deeds of their leaders.[8]

Judgments about leaders are not based on what the leader says, but what he does. When leaders act in moral ways, we are more apt to believe them and entrust them with our loyalty. Most followers appreciate a person who takes an ethical stand on important standards and principles.

The word "integrity" comes from the Latin *integritas*, which means to be whole or complete. Deciding to live a life of integrity will lead to a life of inner peace and inner wholeness. Most people discover, though, after deciding to be people of integrity, that the high values it includes are not easy to maintain. Sooner or later conflict will arise between what they know is right and what seems expedient for profit making or reputation. During political campaigns or in attempts to make that big sale, the truth, kindness, and honesty seem to be left in the dirt of the necessity to win. When leaders use deception to gain trust or support from followers, trust is violated, and it is very difficult for those followers to regain trust in their leaders.

Interactions with others are the most common challenges leaders must face. In every relationship, from friendship to employment to partnership, there will come a time when what one person wants is in direct conflict with what another person wants. How leaders handle such conflicts will reveal their own temperament,

8. Kouzes and Posner, *Leadership Challenge*, 22.

personal character, and control. In a business partnership, when partners see things differently, there must be a means of agreeing upon a solution. Under pressure, leaders exhibiting self-control will not make promises they cannot keep. Co-workers who promise they will take care of an item of business and fail to do so are undermining the integrity of the company. Leaders who allow themselves to display anger when they are thwarted or contradicted, or when someone doesn't agree with them, are simply revealing their own lack of maturity and ability to handle problematic situations. Angry people are obviously focused on themselves—their own desires and needs. Effective leaders do not allow their own egos and emotions to interfere with objective evaluations of what is best for the company. Neither do they allow personal emotional reactions to interfere with their sense of integrity.

How do we ensure that integrity will be a priority in our lives? Aside from simply saying "be honest" and "be truthful," several suggestions come to mind. First, take time to make conscious decisions. Quick solutions may end up hurting someone, so taking time to evaluate the consequences of all possible actions will usually give the best alternative for all concerned. Second, getting advice from others may take extra time, but the results will be worth the time if doing so avoids hurting someone else or keeps us from questionable actions. Integrity demands that we do not act in questionable ways simply to please a boss or client. Taking time may offer the opportunity to come up with a better solution. Third, maintaining integrity in leadership requires that leaders acknowledge and confront any personal habits or tendencies to be sneaky, insensitive, or dishonest. Most people have certain situations that they deal with in less than honest ways. It is easy to lie (a white lie is still a lie), exaggerate, misrepresent, or take advantage of someone else's ignorance or trust in order to advance our own agendas. Such situations need extra effort so that our actions and statements coincide with our commitment to integrity.

Teri Bernstein, professor of Business and Personal Ethics at Santa Monica College in Southern California, has a theory as to why people often compromise their ethics. She suggests that

Moral Leadership

in response to a dilemma people usually will immediately come up with two options—one that is self-sacrificing and one that is self-centered (and may hurt others). She tries to teach students to look for a third option—one that will consider their own needs but also not hurt others. It may take creative thinking to come up with that third option, but such a process will certainly maintain one's integrity.[9]

In making the changes in our lives that moral integrity requires, we must also be aware that such changes may not be popular. When people are used to being praised or flattered, they may not respond positively to being told that their suggestions will not work. If those people turn against the honest leaders, the leaders have more opportunity to show the important traits of respect, humility, problem solving, and a positive attitude.

Author Stuart Crainer gives an example of ethics at work. He reports that Levi-Strauss published an Aspirations Statement in 1987 that challenges all employees to model "new behaviors, empowerment, ethical management practices, and good communications." The Aspiration Statement commits the company to value. Consequently, managers are evaluated according to values as well as performance. To enforce the values, a significant 40 percent of management bonuses are awarded on issues relating to "ethics, values, and personal style in human relations as set out in the Aspiration Statement." Levi-Strauss company president Peter Jacobi states, "We have told our people around the world what we value, and they will hold us accountable. Once you do that, it's like letting the genie out of the bottle. You can't go back."[10] Sometimes the public verbalization of an ethical or moral stand is necessary, or at least helpful, for our own commitment to such practices.

Steven Covey, author of *The Seven Habits of Highly Successful People*, stresses the importance of balance, but also emphasizes a strong inner core of integrity.[11] Sometimes integrity is the necessary balance—it balances the leadership of those powerful

---

9. Felder, *Ten Challenges*, 172–73.
10. Crainer, *The 75 Greatest Management Decisions*, 90–91.
11. Covey, *Seven Habits*.

controllers. Leaders who lie, cannot be trusted to keep promises, break confidences, push boundaries to achieve success, are not exhibiting integrity. Integrity keeps leaders human and personal.

Author Bradford D. Smart, when pointing out that integrity is one of the expected personal competencies for hiring, agrees that integrity is "Ironclad"—in other words, integrity is absolutely essential. He explains that a person with integrity "does not cut corners, ethically. Remains consistent in terms of behavior toward others. Earns trust of coworkers . . . Puts organization's interests above self. Does what is right, not what is politically expedient . . . Does not play games with facts to win a point."[12]

Moral dilemmas are the natural result of trying to lead with integrity and model a moral lifestyle. Leaders who decide not to deal deceitfully with clients or co-workers will not find a simple, easy road ahead of them, but they will find the right road.

A sense of ethics demands business with a conscience. Ethics come naturally to some people—those who live with the idea of community and others and the good of the whole. Other people, though, struggle to operate with ethical actions; it is so much easier to act for self-profit or self-benefit. Regardless of whether moral actions and ethical treatment of people come easily or not, ethics pay. There may be obvious tangible benefits of awards or company loyalty, but even if these do not show up, there is the personal satisfaction of having acted in the right way.

3. VISION

"Unless a man undertakes more than he possibly can do," states Henry Drummond, "he will never do all that he can." Another writer stated that "nothing is as approved as mediocrity. The majority has established it and it fixes its fangs on whatever gets beyond it either way" (Unknown).

Effective leaders tend to have a long-term, future orientation. They look beyond the present day with its problems or successes.

---

12. Smart, *Topgrading*, 377.

Moral Leadership

Vision is the ability to imagine the ideal. Literally, of course, it means "to see." It suggests, though, much more than a physical ability, by making us think of foresight, forward-looking, and future orientation. Vision is an image—a picture of what could be, possibilities, even perhaps the ideal. Therefore, when we say a leader must have vision, we are suggesting a wide range of possibilities. Followers want a leader who understands that things are not perfect, but who believes that they could be better, and that something should be done to change them. Envisioning a future may be a determination to make things better.

A leader who has vision has the ability to look ahead—to have a sense of concern for the future of the business/company. Whether we call this ability a vision, a dream, a calling, a goal, or some other term, leaders must know where they are going if they expect others to follow their leadership. A leader's ability to develop a strategic plan or a long-term goal for the direction of the company will often be the evidence of that leader's ability to envision a future. The Korn/Ferry, Columbia University study of leadership, shows that 98 percent (in the year 2000) ranked "conveys a strong vision of the future" as a quality necessary for leaders, second only to integrity.[13]

The ability to be forward looking doesn't mean the power of ESP. It is the ability to set a desirable destination for the company, group, or community to work toward. Vision is a kind of magnet that provides others with the security of forming their own courses for the future. Followers need their leader to have a well-defined view of the future so that they can feel a part of what the organization becomes in a year, five years, or ten years. If we know where we are going, we can select the proper route to get there. Getting along a day at a time usually gets us only through the day.

Visions of the future are about possibilities, about a desire, perhaps even an ideal future. In this sense, vision overlaps with positive thinking. To envision the possibilities, a leader must be able to think positively, through the objections and negative feedback. Visionary leaders assume anything is possible. When we

13. Korn/Ferry, *Reinventing the CEO*, 90.

The Nine Leadership Traits

envision a new future, we call into action our value systems—the values we would like to see enacted over time.

Visionary plans are statements of destination. It may take years to build a company or clean up crime from a neighborhood. But these things would never happen at all if someone had not had a vision to do so. Visions are what we would like to see happen in the future. A leader of vision will find a way to bring about the reality of that desire. A vision is not a strategic plan. There is a difference between strategic planning and strategic thinking. A vision requires thinking in ways ungoverned by the numbers, while planning requires working with the numbers—with what *is* rather than what *could be.*

It is not enough for a leader to have a vision. In order for a group/organization to bring about the change indicated in the vision, the leader must be able to communicate that vision. The leader must also be able to get the followers and staff to understand and accept and commit to that vision. Leadership is a dialog, not a monologue; to get others to accept the vision, a leader must understand the dreams and desires of the followers. Leaders must develop a shared sense of destiny—only then will the vision be attainable. When others see how their own hopes and aspirations are aligned with the group vision, they will be willing to commit to the shared vision. Those who commit to a shared vision tend to exhibit more job satisfaction, loyalty, productivity, and pride in the organization.

One of the most effective examples of communicating and sharing a vision or a dream took place on August 28, 1963, when Martin Luther King Jr. shared his dream with the world. His speech that day remains one of the most moving ever given because King rooted his dream in the American dream that everyone could identify with—we all want to be free. Fortunately, not every leader needs to have the outstanding oratory skills of Martin Luther King Jr. However, the eloquence is not nearly as important as the sincerity, the shared values, and the collective benefit of the vision. When people, both leaders and followers, have a common purpose, they find meaning together. Peter Senge states that a shared vision "is a force in people's hearts, a force of impressive power."[14]

Sincerity is the key to presenting a vision or any kind of communication. Most people can spot insincerity right away, and leaders should not try to sell an idea unless they are sold on it themselves. A good question to start with is "What do I believe in?" When leaders share their own beliefs, what is in their souls, they are believable and will move others to follow.

Visions for corporations and big businesses are more complex; however, growth will still occur because someone believes it can happen and that same someone sets out to effect a change. Before a future can be predicted, it must be imagined. A leader with a vision begins that imaginative process. Some leaders are naturally imaginative and visionary; others work hard to develop their imaginative, or creative, side. Native American healer and teacher Bear Heart of Albuquerque, New Mexico, in his book *The Wind Is My Mother*, describes a purifying ritual for not only knowing ourselves better but also for developing a sense of vision. Bear Heart explains that the self-knowledge comes through "our meditation known as the 'Vision Quest'—the setting aside of a time and place, alone out in nature, to communicate with a Higher Being, and explore that which is within. A Vision Quest entails many hours of meditation and doing without . . . as "questers" empty themselves of attachments to become ready to receive. Somewhere in that space of time as we are questing, answers come. It's an opportunity to know more about ourselves and the options that we have to choose from in life."[15]

Perhaps most leaders do not have the luxury of spending many hours in meditation. However, the searching of our own creativity and imagination usually takes time to be alone, out from under the ordinary stresses of daily work and life.

Such a quest for vision illustrates the necessity of clearing the mind of preconceived expectations or personal agendas before making a decision about the future of a group. Leaders need to

---

14. Senge, *Fifth Dimension*, 206.
15. Heart and Lankin, *Wind Is My Mother*, 230–32.

envision a future for their groups, but those visions need to reflect what is truly best for the advancement of the company. Deciding what is best for the group as a whole requires objectivity. A physical time away from everyday decision-making pressures may open the way for objectivity. But when such physical removal from a business or company is not possible or practical, at least leaders can mentally pull away from constant nagging pressures and devote some quality brainstorming time to their vision of the future. Objectifying the future vision for the whole will result in higher productivity and loyalty.

Wasn't it Albert Einstein who called imagination the preview of coming attractions? Whatever leaders cannot visualize, they cannot accomplish. Visionaries anticipate the result they would like to see become a reality; then they can work through the steps to accomplish that result. If the leaders have no vision or imagination, the company or group will be in the same place twenty years from now as it is in today. How do leaders become more visionary—get out of the world as it is? One way is to read voraciously. Reading expands our thought processes because many authors present the future in imaginative ways. They should also nurture their own creativity and also encourage new ideas from their employees, co-workers, and followers.

A vision for the future of a company or organization must be understood and realistic. If it is unrealistic or too vague to be tangible, leaders must start over and create a more concrete vision for the future. Also, leaders must be able to judge how much of the future can be made acceptable to the present. Visionaries see the possibilities of the future before those possibilities are obvious to others. Many people may not be ready to accept some future vision that seems intangible and perhaps unrealistic. Therefore, leaders with vision must be astute enough or intuitive enough to decide when and how to present their visions for the future so that others can accept the possibility of that vision. Followers must be able not only to see the vision but also to help bring it to pass. Because visionary leaders see possibilities that do not yet exist, sometimes it is difficult for followers to see the same vision. One way to help explain a vision is the same way hockey star Wayne Gretzky explained his success. He once said that while most players skate to where the puck is, he skates to where it will be. That is a visionary response. Those leaders who have accomplished most have not dealt with the world as it is, but the world as it would be someday. For example, consider Montgomery and Ward, who began a mail-order catalog in 1872, something unheard of at the time.

Vision overcomes. In 1907 Henry Ford said that his aim was "to build a motor car for the great multitude . . . so low in price that no man . . . will be unable to own one." From his point of view, the automobile would be taken for granted—everyone would drive. Bill Gates, in the same way, had a vision of a computer on every desk and in all homes. Both of these men had the vision to see what might be possible, and they worked to make that vision a reality. The key is to look to the future and then invent it. The means of instant communication we take for granted today were figments of imagination and of science fiction just a few years ago. Our futures will be based on the visions we have today.

4. RESPECT

One must respect others before one can consider them as equals, before one can appreciate or love them. Without respect there is no true love or admiration. When leaders respect followers, they are showing consideration for those followers. Consideration is being the kind of person others need you to be, the kind of person who sees value in all other people. In other words, a considerate person is kind, treating others with dignity, and meeting others' needs, which often means doing things leaders are not obligated to do.

Most of us find it easy to be kind to and considerate of our friends and loved ones, but true leaders are kind to their followers even when those followers are not close friends, and in fact might be hostile in attitude. It is easy to let ourselves seek revenge for hostility and assume we do not need to be kind or considerate of those who are not considerate of us. Such an attitude is not worthy of a moral leader. Respect for all people would require the moral leader to be considerate of others regardless of personal feelings about them.

Many people see consideration or kindness as protecting a weaker person from pain, pressure, and penalty. It often seems to mean overlooking the open affront or lawlessness of a fellow human being because it might be inconsiderate to make an issue over something embarrassing. But this human tendency is not true thoughtfulness or consideration of others; it is closer to tolerance, and tolerance implies a kind of higher and lower status (one tolerates those beneath or lower in status). True respect sees others as equals, not as subservient.

Of all the traits of leadership, respect for others is perhaps the most familiar to our everyday lives. This virtue is healing, compassionate, and merciful to others. Respecting others is usually associated with mercy. It is not possible to be respectful without being merciful. And to be merciful is to be considerate. It implies a deep concern for others.

Respect for others is also the disposition to overlook and forgive personal injuries. Instead of vindicating ourselves or sticking up for personal rights, moral leaders are responsible to uphold the standard of selfless consideration. Such respect may cost a great deal. This is more than pretending concern for others; it is, in fact, getting involved with the personal sorrows and pains of others to the point where it may cost us serious inconvenience. Truly respectful people put aside their own personal preferences in order to offer help to another.

The need to respect others is not merely a general encouragement to treat our fellowman better. The whole world is in need of kind consideration, of course; however, leaders need to show a respect and understanding beyond man's greatest capacity on his own. It is both unconscious and spontaneous. We won't even have to think about it. When we are truly respectful of others, we are moved by an impulsive kindness. As compassion is the opposite of self-pity, in the same way true respect for others is the opposite of self-love and pride.

Moral Leadership

At times of crisis, especially, we have situations that instantly give rise to leaders who might otherwise not have taken charge. In moments of crisis, people are often caught in the grip of uncertainty as a paralyzing fear of the unknown overtakes them. But in these riveting seconds of uncertainty and fear, leaders courageously emerge as they make decisions and take appropriate actions on behalf of those requiring immediate assistance. This assistance is consideration for others. It is getting outside one's own fear and self-protection and taking charge of the protection of other people.

A company should work on the specific goal of developing respect for all people, including the promoting of trust, pride, and commitment to the mission of the whole group. Leaders set up a partnership of sorts—an agreement to work together for the common profit and growth of the organization. When leaders recognize and respect the contributions of the employees/followers, then those followers will also recognize contributions by the leaders. Mutual respect leads to mutual recognition. By showing respect to those around and below them in the organizational flow-chart, leaders are building respect for themselves, so that when they ask for higher levels of performance, followers will be willing to comply. When a leader can believe in and respect followers, they in turn will believe in and respect themselves.

How leaders speak to their followers and co-workers can make all the difference in the company's productivity and growth. Leaders should never be insincere, of course, but their genuine words of respect or inquiry will show a desire to treat those followers as worthy human beings. One outstanding example of respect reaping long-range benefits occurred in the life of Episcopal archbishop Desmond Tutu of South Africa who won the Nobel Prize for his long-term efforts against economic and racial policies in his country prior to the 1994 change of government. Tutu, when he was a child, tells of seeing a white man tip his hat to a black woman. Such a thing was totally unheard of in his country. The white man was an Episcopal bishop and the woman was Tutu's mother.[16] One gesture of respect can change a person's life forever.

16. Copenhaver, *To Begin at the Beginning*, 248.

That simple gesture of tipping a hat changed Archbishop Tutu's life forever.

It is usually easy for people to show respect to their bosses. The test of respect is how one relates to those who sweep the floor and repair the water pipes or run errands. Leaders with respect for all will consider the owner of the company and the janitor as equals. The best leaders treat everyone equally—as valued citizens of the world and of the organization. Each day leaders will be given opportunities to offer support or contribute to discouragement. A leader's words make a lasting impression on each person spoken to.

5. FAITH

Having faith in people is essential for appropriate evaluation of their talents and abilities. Believing in people is essential before a leader can see those people as successful and valuable to the company or group as a whole. A leader who has faith in his followers will not accept negative hearsay about those followers without checking and double checking the source and truth of the comments. Such a leader will give that follower a chance regardless of what might appear to be the majority opinion. A leader who believes in his people knows that there may be another majority with the true facts—facts not evident to one group of people. Leaders who have faith in their followers do not judge them on comments by other people; rather, they will ascertain the truth of the matter before making any judgments. Evaluations will be based strictly on performance (past, present and potential future performance), not on others comments. First believe . . . the belief comes before the proof (Anonymous).

Such synonyms as "trust," "faithfulness," "conviction," "integrity," and "fidelity" are often used as alternatives for or translations of *faith*. Thus the word "faithful" is capable of the double meaning of "faith" and "faithfulness." A leader's faith in his followers produces dependability beyond the ordinary.

Along with having faith in others, a moral leader needs to be a faithful person, a faithful leader. Such faithfulness shows commitment to moral ideals. Faithful people are committed to moral firmness, standards of moral duty, principles of right behavior, and esteemed moral attributes. Leaders who have faith in others are themselves faithful because they are acting consistently with their own tenets of life. Having faith in others involves keeping faith with others. True faith manifests dependability in doing the work we are called to do, especially when that work is leading others in an organization or group of any kind.

Having faith in others, believing in them and their ability to accomplish high levels of productivity, requires personal integrity. Without personal integrity, one is suspicious of others. Without personal integrity, it is not possible to believe in others. A leader with integrity has one self, at work and at home, with family and with colleagues. Leaders without integrity, without faith in others, often have one self at home, another at the office, and sometimes even a third or fourth for social or political occasions. Integrity and faith in others demands one self, an honest presentation of self to followers. Such a leader expects this same level of integrity from others, and he will challenge them to follow his example.

Leaders who demonstrate faithfulness usually impact others, by example as well as by actions. When they cannot be with their constituents or followers, they touch them through a deep, abiding certainty of faithfulness and commitment to those followers.

This does not mean leaders are perfect. They make mistakes. They are tempted to judge by appearances rather than by facts. But they do respect and expect consistency. Behavior consistent with beliefs will earn credibility, both for leaders and followers. Such consistency earns believability. When leaders can trust and believe in their followers, progress and growth are not only possible, but certain.

The truly faithful leaders will be faithful in the commonplace things of life, the monotonous routine of the day. They will be just as faithful when, metaphorically, it is raining as when the sun is shining. Both the faithful leader and follower will find the place they are to be for the best of the company, and they will stay there and be faithful in that position.

Faithfulness is a means by which we develop our own characters and a means of making us able to work effectively for our followers.

Having faith in others, believing in others, reaps enormous benefits. Leaders show belief in associates by involving them in problem solving—by asking them questions to get them involved, such as "What problems do we have?" and "What is the best solution?" or "Are there alternative solutions that would benefit more departments?" and "What timeline and costs are available?" As the followers answer the questions with the leader, they become involved in the project, making it their own because they are solving its problems. They also sense the leader's belief in them as they are asked for solutions to problems some leaders might choose to solve alone. This kind of questioning and brainstorming also eliminates many critical feelings or comments about the solution. Because associates are part of the solution, they can see the reasons alternatives won't work as well, and they can accept the most reasonable solution.

On the contrary, if the solution is dictated to them, the followers will undoubtedly think they could offer a better one, giving rise to critical feelings about the chosen answers. Group brainstorming allows everyone to arrive at the same viable alternative, and it shows that the leader believes the group is capable of arriving at the best alternative. A secure leader who believes in associates will give them the freedom to do things their own way, even if it is not exactly the way that leader would act.

When leaders believe followers can perform, those followers gain confidence in their own abilities. This creates a circular process as people respond to the belief and trust invested in them. Studies of this phenomenon, called self-fulfilling prophecy, provide much evidence that people act in ways consistent with others' expectations of them.[17]

---

17. See, for example, works by Jones, Field and Seters, and Dov Eden, (Director of Israel's Institute of Business Research) listed in the Bibliography and Works Cited Appendix.

Thus, if we expect others to succeed, they will. If we expect others to fail, they probably will. For example, when parents make a child feel incapable of any certain action, the child will not be able to perform that action.

People often describe an effective leader as someone who can bring out the best in them. Associates are willing to be led when the one leading wants them to be as successful as possible. Leaders who believe in others are creating a self-fulfilling prophecy. Feeling appreciated improves self-worth, and feelings of self-worth bring about accomplishment and success. Research confirms what all of us have suspected, that people with high self-esteem, regardless of age, gender, educational level, or economic background "feel unique, competent, secure, empowered, and connected to" those around them.[18]

One of the strongest means of building self-esteem in employees/followers is for employers/leaders to believe in the abilities of their followers, having faith in their abilities to accomplish whatever needs to be done. Only those who envision themselves as winners, as successful, will work hard enough not only to become winners, but to become leaders themselves.

Of all the traits of a moral leader, faithfulness may be the most inconspicuous. The faithful person is usually taken for granted. Nevertheless, faithfulness is one of the most necessary virtues. The reliability of people shows in related attributes of loyalty, honesty, and integrity. Such a person is faithful in words, in actions, and in character. Such a person is trustworthy. Trust is the foundation of leadership. Leaders cannot take shortcuts regardless of how long they have been leaders. To build trust, leaders must lead with competence, character, and consideration.

Leaders know that customers will deal with a company they trust. In like manner, that company has the responsibility to maintain that trust by not letting the customers down. Leaders operate the same way—they know that followers will follow someone they trust. And leaders have the responsibility not to violate the trust employees/followers have in them. Leaders must have a consistent

---

18. Blitzer, et al, "Build Self-Esteem," 1993.

value system so that they will not violate that trust. There must also be some tolerance for imperfection—neither the leaders nor the followers are perfect. As leaders exercise tolerance in dealing with followers, their followers will try to live up to the trust placed in them. Therefore, belief or trust works both ways—one must be a trustworthy person and also trust others.

Belief should never change. The basic truth of people and the organization's foundation must remain strong if the organization is to survive. The world changes, the product changes, and even the way the company operates may change. Nevertheless, the basic ethical beliefs of a company or group, and their basic belief in their people should remain strong. Faith in people shows most clearly through the close, consistent, and compassionate consideration of the feelings and needs of others.

6. PERSEVERANCE

Perseverance shows up many ways. A leader who perseveres will not only continue to work to achieve the company's goals, but will also exhibit patience when dealing with followers. Having patience means calmly working for the desired results in spite of negative circumstances.

Persevering is often equated with patience, for they are much alike and function in much the same way. Patience is the powerful capacity to suffer long under adversity. It is the ability to bear with difficult people or with adverse circumstances without breaking down. It allows people to remain steadfast under strain, not just standing still, but pressing on. Patience is being able to bear up under suffering or despair. A leader with patience exhibits self-restraint in the face of unsatisfied desire.

Outstanding leaders are patient with their teams. Leaders show patience while others are acquiring skills, and they allow time for others to reach specified goals. Patience enables people to get to their destinations, pursue their dreams, and leave obscurity behind. Both leaders and followers patiently practice their skills to remain on the cutting edge. As they exercise their skills and arrive at competitive levels of expertise, the playing field will level out for them.

In addition, it is important that leaders instill patience within those they lead. Doing so will help their followers accomplish the team's mission. The results will be greater success and higher productivity. These factors translate into greater rewards or promotions from supervisors and greater growth for the group as a whole.

Persevering leaders are not always understood and do not necessarily have a clear path ahead of them to accomplish whatever they wish. Sometimes followers and co-workers who do not understand the goal or vision may try to derail the process. One of the most difficult lessons for the maturing leader (or follower) is how to react to unjust treatment. Misunderstanding and mistreatment will follow the moral leader just as they follow anyone else on earth. So, while we can count on not being treated rightly, the issue is how we will react when we are treated wrongly. Trouble affects people in one of two opposite ways: it can either make them bitter or make them tender. Our jobs as leaders is to emerge from problems and trouble with tenderness intact and our followers in mind.

Some of us are willing to suffer a time of trouble in order to gain success as great leaders. But we want to have problems for only a short time. We certainly do not want to have to endure problems for long periods of time. Very often, it is the endurance or the suffering through trouble that brings the perseverance. Perseverance, like patience, is not an instantaneous gift—it is developed over time and with painful experiences. Without perseverance and patience, we are incomplete. A sense of perseverance or patience can transform the hardest leadership experience into a positive experience as we begin to see the purpose beyond the present problem.

Sometimes leaders find it difficult to persevere and stick to their goals. It is difficult to stay open and committed when the end of a long-term project is not clearly in sight. Frustrations are common whenever projects or goals are not accomplished immediately or on schedule. Some leaders tend to want results yesterday or before. Leaders who allow frustrations to erupt into anger and recriminations aimed at followers will find that they are losing the trust and loyalty of some of their followers. But leaders who remain calm, stay with the plan, and continue to practice their positive thinking skills, will eventually see the result they have planned for. Setbacks and delays are not opportunities for anger, revenge, or bitterness. Rather, they are opportunities and challenges for creative persistence.

Perseverance requires self-discipline. Most successful leaders are self-starters, able to begin and carry through projects without being told to do so. Many leaders are also self-disciplined. However, self-discipline is not the same as well disciplined. The military needs well-disciplined people—people who can carry out orders under duress. However, in other parts of our business and social worlds, the self-discipline of being able to take the initiative and accomplish the company's goals even when there is no one giving orders may be even more important. Self-disciplined people tend to be individualistic in their responsibility and commitment to the organization as a whole. They tend to be people who will persevere until the job is completed.

People who have accomplished unusual things in life have had an undeviating belief in themselves, but also they have continued to try again and again after apparent failure. Peter Burwash, author of a short book called *The Key to Great Leadership*, has a two-page chapter on perseverance. He cites three examples of persevering behavior that are extremely pertinent. Thomas Edison, reports Burwash, had 1,350 unsuccessful attempts at creating the light bulb, and yet kept trying. Albert Einstein said, "I think and think for months and years. Ninety-nine times, the conclusion is false. The hundredth time I am right." Federal Express founder Fred Smith received a C in his economics class for the paper that outlined the ideas for an overnight delivery service. His professor said it was okay, but it wouldn't work.[19] Persevering leaders believe in themselves and their dreams. Even when others say it can't be done, they do not give up.

The benefits of perseverance are many. Perseverance produces within our characters tremendous strength and endurance,

---

19. Burwash, *Key to Great Leadership*, 42.

even toughness. It brings the toughness that allows us to endure difficult people and hard situations with serenity and stability. When we persevere under adversity, we become aware that we are even more able to handle adversity and tough situations. Leaders who persevere in their relationships with their followers show that they value those who follow. Putting others' concerns before one's own concerns shows perseverance and selflessness. Such traits indicate a powerful leader.

7. HUMILITY

What is humility? And why is it important to leadership? Humility is not the action or habit of putting one's self down or pretending not to be equal with other people; neither is it fake self-abasement. Most people think that the "humble" person has no self-confidence, and certainly that person would not be one to follow. However, that is not really what a humble person is at all. According to Confucius, "The superior man is modest in his speech, but exceeds in his actions."

Humility needs a place in our everyday lives. Often referred to as "gentleness" or "meekness," the word *humility* has a more positive connotation than the other words. Many think of the meek or humble person as weak and ineffective, even applying those words only to people who are physically weak or emotionally ineffective. But this concept of weakness is contrary to the gentleness and sensitivity we see in the humility of the greatest leaders. Gentle actions are not the result of weak backbone. Gentleness and humility are expressions of power under perfect control. A humble leader is an effective leader because followers know they can expect and receive recognition for their own worth from that leader. They know he will not take advantage of his position to exploit them or use them unfairly.

The opposite of humility would be hardness of heart. We must not let hardness of heart creep into our attitudes. Hard heartedness will separate us from those we lead and keep us from treating people with value and respect. Many people want to lead; not

The Nine Leadership Traits

many want to follow. But the personal, sensitive, humble leader will know his own place and be successful in getting others to follow.

True humility is contrary to human nature and the ways of our world. We like to have the upper hand, to be in charge. We like to say the last word; we like for people to applaud us. We like power. That is the reason we all like to be leaders. However, the sensitive, humble person will work for the good of others rather than for self-advancement. The sensitive, humble leader will work for the good of the organization and the people who comprise that organization, even if it means giving up personal comfort or personal glory. This kind of action demonstrates true leadership. There will never be hard feelings where there is real sensitivity to others. A completely humble self cannot be offended.

One attractive thing about sincere moral leaders is the spirit of sensitivity and personal interest they exude. Humility in our characters does not show in the way our voices sound or the expressions on our faces. Instead, it is the spirit in which a conversation or meeting or business deal is shared. The main focus is that people will be treated equally. We can conquer people by argument, but never convert them by argument. It takes the genuine character of moral leadership to convert a follower. If we consider others as valuable, it is easy to be humble and sensitive to them and their needs.

Humility gives a leader a sense of peace—there is no need to be constantly competitive and constantly worrying about who may or may not be getting ahead in the market. Peace leads to the most tranquil leaders, and therefore is a reasonable sub-point of leadership traits. An effective leader must be at peace to put others at ease. One can have inner peace, regardless of circumstances. It is not based on peace treaties and the cessation of war. As desirable as these are, treaties bring neither lasting peace nor an inner rest to the spirit of humankind. Regardless of external circumstances, the spirit of humankind will be vexed and distraught without good qualities calming the raging sea inside. Peace is a part of moral and ethical character; therefore it is intended to be a witness of morality in social interaction. Actually, the role of a "peacemaker" should not be restricted to the reconciliation of those at variance, though all leaders must do that at times.

There will undoubtedly be rough times, but when leaders remain calm during tough times, they exude peaceful demeanors, which will calm others. Without the sense of peace that humble leaders usually have, many leaders would succumb to fear. Since leaders are at the top of their hierarchy, they carry more responsibilities, and they must be at peace with themselves to have the greatest impact on those they lead. The kind of peace that leaders need is the secure and confident repose of the soul in themselves. The leader has composure of spirit in all circumstances because he is insulated, not from troubles, but from the anxiety that usually accompanies those troubles.

In terms of leadership, peace is often contrasted with fear. If one is not peaceful in a position of leadership, the cause may be fear of the circumstances or of the self or of those waiting to be led. A good leader must remember that fear is often accompanied with pride. Pride, a henchman of fear, masks wisdom, sound judgment, and servanthood with a self-serving arrogance. Most fearful leaders are also proud, which in turn leads to poor organizations, underachieving teams, and poor performances. When leaders find themselves fearful, it is especially important to enter into the peace available for them through a humble attitude toward themselves.

Personal egotism blindsides a leader to the realities around him. Actually, such egotism leads leaders to believe they can do no wrong; thus they become menaces to workers in their organizations. This kind of egotism is not the same as normal pride or self-esteem. All leaders must have self-esteem and pride, or self-confidence, in their abilities. All corporate leaders must exert their own personalities in order to motivate people to an objective. Even the most humble leaders have a strong sense of personal ability and self-confidence. However, each leader must also be willing to admit a mistake should one occur. Leaders must be willing to listen to other opinions. One of the best ways to be willing to listen is for leaders to remember their own humble beginnings, their own mistakes of the past, and be open to other points of view and criticisms. Above all, such leaders must be realistic—aware of and sensitive to their followers, welcoming ideas and information, putting self in the perspective of the good of the company.

Some business executives become so caught up in public recognition that they neglect their leadership in the company. These actions are mostly ego massaging. For example, consider a hypothetical leader who became so excited about the kind of scientific management he practiced that he began spending hours and days traveling around making speeches on the subject. He might be widely quoted in the press. But he would be neglecting his own company. His ego was taking over, and his company would get rid of him. Such actions and attitudes are certainly not based in humility. When personal vanity takes over, leaders become victims of their own egotism. Consequently, they lose common sense and objectivity, resulting in bad decisions and fractured relationships.

Having self-esteem and confidence and seeking praise and adulation are two separate things. Secure leaders, or humble leaders, can admit their own errors, even publicly; however, an egotistic leader will never let another seem to have precedence. The line between self-identity and egotism seems very fine, and such distinction may be difficult to explain, but those who work with either the egotist or the secure leader can sense the difference. Egotism creates alienation; self-confidence and humility create loyalty.

Some famous person once said, "People with humility do not think less of themselves, they just think of themselves less." Whoever said it showed great insight into the characteristic of humility. Humble people are not extra weak or self-deprecating. They are strong—strong enough not to need the glory and the credit for accomplishments. Because their egos are not on trial, they can quietly accomplish much more than those who need public acclamation for every success. Leaders with humility do not categorize tasks or people as above or below them. For example, college athletes have been indulged and catered to so much that they often begin to think they are better than the "regular" college students, and therefore they should not have to be responsible for unimportant

Moral Leadership

things such as tests and grades. They should be allowed to graduate simply because they play ball. That is not an attitude of humility. An athlete who plays his best yet still gives credit to the rest of the team and to the coach and tries to abide by the institutional rules is the humble athlete who balances skill with life.

Humility is a major part of a leader's attitude. Mahatma Gandhi spoke often of humility; he once said "the hour of the greatest triumph is the hour of the greatest humility." Many things test a leader's character, but probably nothing tests it more than those opportunities to respond with arrogance or humility.

8. POWER

Abraham Lincoln once said that to test a man's character, give him power. And we are all familiar with the saying that power corrupts and absolute power corrupts absolutely. However power has positive sides too, and it is certainly essential to outstanding moral leadership. Power means many things to different people. Some think of power as the ability to dominate all others. Some think of it as the beginning of abuse. Others see power as the means to an end—the only means to an end. However, the power a leader needs is the power of control, of charisma, and of serving others.

True power allows a leader to empower others to be leaders. Kenneth Blanchard defines empowerment well: Empowerment is all about letting go so that others can get going. Powerful leaders give their own power away, making each person feel capable and powerful.[20]

To understand how a leader can use power to the advantage of his company or group, we must first understand how power works and the various types of power one can or should utilize. The question arises as to the reason some people seem to have much more power than others, or why some people do not seem to have any power at all. We are not able to discuss all the sociological or psychological ramifications of such power struggles, but we will

---

20. Drucker, *Managing for the Future*, 318.

give a brief description of the various types of power, along with sources and theories.

Types and Sources of Power

Depending on how minutely detailed one wishes to be, the kinds of power different people exert seem to be too many to count or to list. The most common types of power, those we see almost every day, would include those listed below. Also, sources of power vary and often overlap with the kinds/types of power. Power may be acquired through various means, such as the following:

- Delegated authority—as in the democratic process.
- Social class or position, especially in certain groups or countries.
- Personal or group charisma—some people have or exude more charisma.
- Influence or tradition—acting on perceived or assumed abilities.
- Expertise, ability, or skills—such as the power of medicine to bring health, or the famous saying that "in the land of the blind, a one one-eyed man is king."
- Persuasion—direct, indirect, or subliminal persuasion might also include religion and politics and moral ideas and areas.
- Knowledge—which may be associated with expertise, but is not the same—may be granted, withheld, shared, or kept secret, but there is no question that knowledge is power.
- Money—financial influence, control of labor, control through ownership is indisputable.
- Force, usually negative, is associated with violence but also with military might and some types of coercion. Is there a positive way to use force?

- Operation of group dynamics—such as the science of public relations.

Theories of Power

The theory of power is a major field of study, and volumes have been written about it. Since it is impossible to discuss even a small portion of such a discipline in a short section, let us look cursorily at some of the major ideas of power that might apply to a leader. Leaders, of course, lead because of the power they have or exert—and that power may be legitimate or not, may be positive or negative, may have come through the leader's own efforts or as a result of nothing the leader has done or said. Some leaders fall into power; others work their way into it.

Friedrich Nietzsche provided a theory of power that underlies much of twentieth century analysis of power. Nietzsche disseminated ideas on the "will to power," which he saw as the domination of other human beings as much as the exercise of control over one's environment. Some leaders develop their own will to power—working themselves into a power position.

Schools of psychology vary in their views of the theory of power, notably the school associated with Alfred Adler, which places power dynamics at the core of the theory, whereas orthodox Freudians might place sexuality at the center. Wherever the drive comes from, most powerful people will admit that there is a drive within them that pushed them on to higher levels of power.

Game theory, with its foundations in the theory of rational choice, is increasingly used in various disciplines to help analyze power relationships. One rational choice definition of power is given by Keith Dowding in his book *Power*. Such a theory is especially relevant to large corporations and companies with multi-level leadership structures.

In rational choice theory, individual humans or groups can be modeled as "actors" who choose from a "choice set" of possible actions in order to try to achieve desired outcomes. An actor's "incentive structure" comprises its beliefs about the costs associated with different actions in the choice set, and the likelihoods that different actions will lead to desired outcomes. The theory allows us to differentiate between two kinds of power: outcome power—the ability of a leader (actor) to bring about or help bring about outcomes, and social power—the ability of a leader (actor) to change the incentive structures of other people (other actors) in order to bring about outcomes.

This framework of rational choice can be used to model a wide range of social interactions where people have the ability to exert power over others. For example, a "powerful" person can take options away from another's choice sets, can change the relative costs of actions, can change the likelihood that a given action will lead to a given outcome, or might simply change the other's beliefs about its incentive structure. A threat of violence can change the likely costs and benefits of different actions, so can a financial penalty in a "voluntarily agreed" contract or a friendly offer.

One of the broader modern views of the importance of power in human activity comes from the work of Michel Foucault, who said, "Power is everywhere . . . because it comes from everywhere."[21] Foucault's works analyze the link between power and knowledge. He outlines a form of covert power that works *through* people rather than only *on* them. Foucault claims belief systems gain momentum, and hence power, as more people come to accept the particular views associated with that belief system as common knowledge. Such belief systems define their figures of authority, such as medical doctors or priests in a church. Within such a belief system—or discourse—ideas crystallize as to what is right and what is wrong, what is normal and what is deviant. Within a particular belief system, certain views, thoughts, or actions become unthinkable. These ideas, being considered undeniable "truths" come to define a particular way of seeing the world, and the particular way of life associated with such truths becomes normalized. He says, "One needs to be nominalistic, no doubt; power is not an institution, and not a structure; neither is

21. Foucault, *History of Sexuality*, 93.

it a certain strength we are endowed with; it is the name that one attributes to a complex strategic situation in a particular society.

Domination is not always the global kind of domination that one person exercises over others, or that one group imposes on another group, says Foucault discussing the manifold forms of domination that can be exercised within society.[22] He continues, "The analysis [of power] should not attempt to consider power from its internal point of view and . . . should refrain from posing the labyrinthine and unanswerable question: 'Who then has power and what has he in mind? What is the aim of someone who possesses power?'"[23] Instead of seeing power that way, we need to see power as a case of studying at the point where its intention, if it has one, is completely invested in its real and effective practices.[24] We want to know the motivations behind one's power—why is one person leading, and is that leadership more effective than another person's leadership?

If our behaviors, our time, and our resources are subjected to power that controls us, even to a minor extent, we should discover how it is that the organization wants or seeks to obtain that control.

The seminal work of Steven Lukes was developed from a talk he was invited to give in Paris. In this brief book, Lukes outlines two dimensions through which power had been theorized in the earlier part of the twentieth century (note dimensions one and two below) which he critiqued as being limited to those forms of power that could be seen. To these he added a third "critical" dimension that built upon insights from Gramsci and Althusser. In many ways this work evolved alongside of the writing of Foucault and serves as a good introduction to his thoughts on power.

One-dimensional power[25] is

- Decision making

- Exercised in formal institutions

22. Ibid., 96.
23. Ibid., 97.
24. Ibid.
25. Lukes, *Power*, 15.

The Nine Leadership Traits

- Measured by the outcomes of decisions.

In his own words, Lukes states that the one-dimensional view of power involves a focus on behavior in the making of decisions on issues over which there is an observable conflict of subjective interests, seen as express policy preferences, revealed by political participation.

Two-dimensional power[26] is all of the items in one-dimensional power plus it includes:

- Decision making and agenda setting
- Measurement of informal influence
- Institutions and informal influences

Techniques used by two-dimensional power structures include: influence, authority, inducement, coercion, persuasion, direct force, and manipulation.

Three-dimensional power[27] includes all aspects of models one and two. Plus it also

- Shapes preferences via values, norms ideologies.
- Says all social interaction involves power because ideas operate behind all language and action.
- Is not obviously measurable: we must infer its existence (focus on language).
- Shows ideas or values that ground all social and political activity, e.g., religious ideas (Christianity, secularism, etc.); self-interest for economic gain.
- Allows these to become routine—we do not consciously think of them.
- Sees political ideologies as informing policy making without being explicit, e.g., neo-liberalism.[28]

26. Ibid., 20.
27. Ibid. 24.
28. Lukes, *Power*, 25.

Moral Leadership

In organizations we usually think of power as the control over resources—over people, money, progress, and outcomes. The more control someone has, the more powerful that person is.

Facts are power. Leaders must ask straight questions and get straight answers. Without facts, accurate information, leaders cannot make the best decisions for the group. Leaders also know that facts obtained from people are only as reliable as the reliability of the person giving the facts. Facts are seldom truly facts; they are what people think are facts, and they may be loaded with assumptions. To maintain power, leaders must do the homework of verification. It is not acceptable to shift the blame for poor information on those who do not make the decisions.

Power is multi-faceted. One facet is learning to delegate. Leaders who need to personally dot every "i" and cross every "t" are not exhibiting more power, but less. Giving up control in specific areas will increase team spirit and loyalty and thus increase production. Jane Wollman Rusoff, in her article "Making the Team Work" quotes Mike Swenson, senior consultant with Swenson Financial Advisory Group at Piper Jaffray. Swenson states that unequivocally, "second guessing your . . . team just isn't productive" Rusoff adds that a good leader "needs to park his ego in the parking lot." And she supports the statement by quoting a team partner, CFP Doug McDaniel: "It's important that the lead person be one who can demonstrate humility by thinking about the good of the partnership."[29] Powerful leaders have to realize that not everyone will do things their way, but that is all right. Giving up a little control in one area will increase control overall by expanding it to many areas. Powerful leaders will maintain the balance between power and humility, which is essential for all successful leaders.

Effective leaders understand and act on the paradox of power. That paradox is that we become more powerful as we give our power away. Leaders acquire power from those they lead rather than from titles or positions they might hold. Power is not a fixed commodity—it does not come in fixed amounts so that if we give some away, we will have less. Instead, power is amorphous—it

29. Rusoff, *Research*, 42–46.

grows in effectiveness as it is shared. Shared power results in higher job satisfaction and performance. When leaders share power, they show trust in, and respect for, their followers. When leaders believe in followers, those followers tend to believe in themselves. Successful leaders thus use their own power to serve others rather than to serve self. Sharing power develops competence, offers visible support, and ensures self-leadership among associates.

Why does one person in an organization seem to have more power than others? Power comes from various sources, including expertise, information, status, or control of resources. Some people wield disproportionate power through special authority, extra expertise, or sheer force of personality. Power often requires a balance with other, more person-oriented, traits. Balance would include proper interaction between the leaders' responsibilities at home and at work, between relationships, friendships, hobbies, and other interests or activities. Balance will help leaders to avoid burnout as well as avoid unreasonable demands from any one area of life.

9. ATTITUDE

A leader must have positive or possibility thinking—a desire to see things happen; but even more than that, a leader needs the belief that things can happen, can improve, can grow. Although a leader must also be a critical thinker, it is important not to squelch every idea by pointing out the reasons such an idea would never work. Realistically, a leader evaluates each new idea, sees the possible problems, but also sees the possible successes, and is willing to take appropriate chances for those successes. Going to the limit, or going beyond what has been done before, takes a group beyond run-of-the-mill achievements and puts them in the new frontiers of innovation. A positive attitude will help a leader overcome the criticism of others who say "It can't be done" or "It's never been done before." A leader's positive attitude allows an organization or group to accomplish new things and experience growth and advancement in new areas.

Moral Leadership

All new ventures begin with possibility thinking, not probability thinking. Positive leaders will assume that anything is possible, and this belief will sustain them when problems arise. Problems can defeat leaders and associates who are not ready to meet them with positive approaches of solution.

A positive attitude includes being generally optimistic, which means to take delight in life. Optimism is not to be confused with happiness. Happiness is a feeling based on positive circumstances, but it dissipates when these circumstances worsen. Happiness comes from an old English word *hap,* and is related to the word *happened.* Happiness is produced by an outside event, by external causes; it is the product of circumstances or what has happened. Thus, it cannot be enduring. Optimism is much more than happiness. It is a decision of the will to see the positive side of things regardless of the circumstances. Optimism should also be distinguished from natural joy. Natural joy is cheerfulness, contentment, or mirth, and is usually associated with the attainment of a desired goal—as satisfaction. But an ongoing optimistic spirit has nothing to do with such external stimulation. Optimism is based on a trait of character that allows leaders to see the best possible outcomes and also see the best in others; they see possibilities when negative people see only failure or disappointment.

We can have positive attitudes that are not dependent on circumstances—we can be filled with optimism even when we are facing difficult times with family or with the businesses we run. The implication is that optimism is permanent and ongoing—that it remains with leaders and with all of us, regardless of circumstances around us. Of course it is much more difficult to be optimistic after a set-back or failure, but optimism is not genuine unless it can meet adversity.

It is essential to look at the positive side of circumstances and have faith that negative things will work out for the good of everyone—to believe that meaning can be found in any event and we can take pleasure in its value.

People enjoy being around optimistic people; it magnetizes others and draws them to its source. One cannot overestimate the

The Nine Leadership Traits

power of a positive outlook. Optimism may be the most expressive leadership trait. And it creates the charisma that might otherwise be lacking in one's personality.

Optimism is a vital source of strength. It gives strength for the ordinary tasks of life, for the trials of life, and for what may seem to be humiliating service. Optimism can be a resource in overcoming the temptation to complain about fellow employees, customers, or situations that seem unfair. In fact, optimism can be as effective as medicine for rejuvenating the body and soul and for giving energy to work through the struggles of leadership.

Positive-thinking leaders challenge the ongoing processes of business by searching for opportunities to change. They believe the future can be better than the present. Positive thinkers look for ways to improve. They take risks. They learn from disappointments. The type of leadership provided makes a definite difference in performance and in long-term health.[30] Leaders who provide followers with a positive sense of direction will encourage them to do their best. A leader's positive view of the present and the future will inspire the group to make the seemingly impossible actually be possible, and to see that what only seems possible can become reality.

How do leaders convince people to succeed, to complete difficult tasks? By making those followers believe they can do those difficult things. Positive-thinking leaders exude energy and are convinced that followers have the power to accomplish whatever they desire. They pass along that conviction to their followers, who then begin believing in themselves as doers of the impossible.

Speaking positively is a key to positive thinking. Positive-thinking leaders say "will" and "can" rather than "try." Also, rather than dwelling on the hardships or problems of an action (why it will not work), positive leaders dwell on the possibility of success (why it will work). Of course, positive thinkers do not ignore objections and problems; realistic evaluation is key to any successful problem solving. But the focus is on possibilities, not impossibilities. Inspiring leaders are possibility thinkers, not probability thinkers.

---

30. Peterson and Bossio, *Health and Optimism*, 1991.

Enthusiasm is catching. Positive leaders usually show enthusiasm in words and in action. Of course, those leaders must sincerely believe in the ideas presented. Any leader who is not excited about the new idea, or who does not believe in its success, will not be able to convince followers to believe in it either.

Many studies have been conducted on the importance of self-talk, or what we tell ourselves about ourselves. Negative thinkers reinforce their own behavior and attitudes by telling themselves things like "no way, it can't be done, never been done before, that would be too hard or take too long, or dumb idea." Positive thinkers, however, allow for possibilities as they tell themselves things such as "can do, yes, that could be possible, why not? let's give it a try, or I think that might work." Unfortunately, there are usually more people around us who will say "it can't be done" than those who say it can be done. At one time, someone said, "Man fly? No Way!" and "That machine can remember what I type? Ridiculous!" Possibility thinkers realize that people will follow when someone knows the goal and leads the way.

Positive thinkers usually are positive about life as a whole. Positive attitudes are usually associated with enthusiasm—a zest for life and for the work of leadership. Enthusiasm causes others to want to follow. Positive mental attitudes are contagious, encouraging others through praise, belief, and trust. Positive thinkers are not concerned with boosting their own egos, so they can easily celebrate others' successes, thereby showing belief in them and building trust. Possibility thinkers do not see problems as deterrents and blockages but as questions that need to be answered. Rev. Robert Schuller, long-time pastor of Crystal Cathedral in Garden Grove, California, is famous for saying, "It is better to attempt something and fail, than to attempt nothing and succeed."

In the movie *Apollo 13*, when the astronauts were trapped in the spaceship on their mission to the moon, the crew could not solve the problem and mission control in Houston did not know what to do. Nevertheless, the flight director in Houston said the goal of the mission was to bring the three crewmen back safely.

He said something that allowed mission control to come up with a solution. He simply said, "Failure is not an option."

The first step to overcoming problems is not to accept failure. Positive thinkers keep looking ahead with success-oriented perspectives, with long-range objectives that can and will succeed. The leader's drive to succeed is a powerful motivator. It must be accompanied with adaptability, however, for if one strategy does not work, the positive leader needs to create another. Staying with a plan that doesn't work is short-sighted, but being able to adjust and adapt to a new way of achievement shows possibility thinking.

Change can be difficult. It is especially difficult for negative thinkers because they tend to believe any change will be for the worse. However, thinking positively about change will focus energy on progress and growth rather than problems. Change is much easier when it is looked at positively. A positive approach gives opportunities to begin again. It allows opportunities to learn from the mistakes of the past and grow from those experiences. Positive thinking is a matter of perception—what matters most is how we look at things. When a problem or a change presents itself, a good response would be, "What am I supposed to learn from this?" Such a response is a great example of positive thinking because it focuses on the good that can come from any negative situation. How things affect us depends largely on us—on how we react to those situations. The situation may not be so bad if we do not see it as negative.

Norman Vincent Peale taught people to see possibilities—no matter how dark things look or seem to be, he encouraged us to lift our vision and see possibilities, for they are always there. Almost every situation in our lives is an opportunity. The negative thinker would call it a chance for something to go wrong. But a positive thinker would see it as an opportunity for something good to happen, an opportunity for growth or service. Instead of complaining about a situation, look for a solution. Complaining doesn't accomplish anything. Do you remember reading about Edison complaining about the darkness? Or the Wright brothers complaining about not being able to fly? Remember what John

Moral Leadership

Wooden, famous basketball coach, said to his team about not letting what they could not do interfere with what they could do. Wooden focused on the positive, not talking about winning as much as working hard and doing their best. That positive attitude led to a record number of championships for his team and a winning attitude for his team members.

Summary of the Nine Leadership Traits

Effective leaders do not lead because they have to but because they want to. They do not calculate what they can get out of a situation, but act spontaneously, not telling others what to do but showing the way. Poor leaders create divisions by pitting one follower against another, are out only for themselves, indulge in putting others down to exalt themselves, despise interference from true authority above them, and will say anything that sounds good whether it is true or not.

Leaders can learn much from children. For several decades, the French ethnologist Hubert Montagner studied gestural language in children. He developed a system for classifying how children relate non-verbally to each other. He came up with five categories:

1. Attractive actions
2. Threatening actions
3. Aggressive actions
4. Gestures of fear and restriction
5. Actions that produce isolation

Montagner found that children who became leaders used attractive actions, not aggressive or threatening ones. The natural leaders were not the young hitters, pinchers, yellers, pullers, or bullies, but rather those who offered toys, smiled, clapped hands, extended a hand, and spoke softly.[31] Consequently, Montagner

---

31. Pines, *Psychology Today*, 58–65.

showed that warmth and friendship attracts followers much more than does aggression.

A leader leads his people; a commander commands them. Commanders usually rule by fear—by their attitudes, actions, and words, such as, "I want this done by this date or heads will roll!" The leaders of companies should realize that people are not working *for* them, but *with* them; they are working both for themselves and for the company as a whole. Effective leaders will help fill the workers' needs as much as they fill their own. Leadership is a sharing process.

Looking back at all nine traits of a successful moral leader, and looking for a term that would encompass all of those traits, nothing seems more appropriate than "love," the kind of brotherly love that puts others first. Love may also be the key ingredient to outstanding leadership. Leaders who want to succeed must show the concern and respect for their followers that also can be described as a kind of love. That love may be for the organization or the work as a whole, but it is essential to the relationship between people. Leaders love their followers in the sense that they care what happens to them. This kind of non-physical, unselfish love will remain firm when the last selfish act, the last cruel ambition, the last deed of hate has been done. Love lies at the root of all true nobility, goodness, or heroism. Leaders grow in love for others as they grow in character and learn to be moral leaders. Although followers may be able to overlook slips in competence in their leaders, they will not so easily forgive lapses in character or lack of consideration of others. General Norman Schwarzkopf once said, "Leadership is a potent combination of strategy and character. But if you must be without one, be without strategy."

Conclusion

Author Peter Drucker points out that effective leadership does not depend on charisma or on any specific leadership qualities. Highly effective leaders such as Franklin D. Roosevelt, Winston Churchill, Douglas MacArthur, and Lenin do not share any leadership

Moral Leadership

qualities or easily-identifiable traits. Instead, states Drucker, leadership is work—Julius Caesar, General MacArthur, Field Marshall Montgomery, or Alfred Sloan (who built and led General Motors from 1920 to 1955) all stress the hard work of thinking through their mission, setting goals and priorities, and maintaining high standards.[32] All of these tasks require consistent hard work. Leaders must see their role as a responsibility rather than a privilege.

Harry Truman's "the buck stops here" is an accurate definition for successful leaders. Consequently, leaders want strong associates. The failures of the followers are the leader's failures, but that leader can also claim the followers' successes. Obviously, then, effective leaders earn the trust of their followers through integrity and consistency. However, one other attribute may be even more important. In order to put in the long hours and hard work necessary to get things done, leaders must have their hearts in their work. Perhaps successful leaders are led by love more than we realize. If so, leadership may be an affair of the heart, rather than of the head.

Many leaders in various avenues of leadership use the word "love" freely when they speak of their motivations to be leaders. The word *encourage* comes from the Latin root *cor*, meaning "heart." When we encourage others, we are giving them heart. When leaders give heart, they are giving love. Vince Lombardi, well-known coach of the Green Bay Packers, believed in love. He made a speech before the American Management Association, in which he said, "Mental toughness is humility, simplicity, spartanism. And one other thing—love. I do not necessarily have to like my associates, but as a person I must love them. Love is loyalty. Love is teamwork. Love respects the dignity of the individual. Heart power is the strength of your corporation."[33]

Retired General H. Norman Schwarzkopf also believed in the power of love. Barbara Walters, in a *20/20* TV interview in 1991, asked him how he would like to be remembered, and Schwarzkopf replied that he would like people to know "that he loved his family,

---

32. Drucker, *Managing for the Future*, 120–21.
33. Peters and Austin, *Passion for Excellence*, 290.

that he loved his troops, and that they loved him." Remember, even though traits mentioned as "leadership traits" may not state specifically any connection with developing the heart, mind, or soul of a leader—where real people reside, real leaders will become aware of the real people working for and with them. People are the greatest asset any leader can have. And successful leaders will cultivate, respect, believe in, and honor that asset above all other concerns in whatever business or group they lead.

four

Effectiveness of the Moral Leader

LEADERSHIP IS THE SKILL of influencing and directing people to accomplish a mission. Leadership goes further than holding power positions. It is being implicitly influential and diplomatically directive while serving. So let's analyze these two traits of influencing and directing to see how they affect leadership.

INFLUENCE

Influence is a force affecting a person or a thing. There are two types of influence—external and internal. External influence is an outside force beyond one's control. Internal influence is an inner force usually within one's control. Leaders are external agents. So one key to leadership is becoming internal to people through influence.

Leaders become internal to people when they help them understand reasons for change. When they give people time to absorb concepts behind change, involve them in decision-making processes, and show they have their best interests at heart (relationship), leaders capture those people's interest, support, and

Effectiveness of the Moral Leader

motivation. Leaders who do this have mastered one of the most powerful leadership tools—influence.

DIRECTING

Leaders influence people by directing effectively. Relationships determine appropriate directing techniques and leaders must tailor directing to the situation. Commanders might say, "I want three sailors on deck for cleanup detail immediately." But ministers might get a similar job done by asking, "Would each of you be so kind as to assist in cleaning the premises after the service?" One scenario involves a paid employee, the other a volunteer.

Directing is exercising proper authority in determining another's course of action. When leaders and subordinates work interdependently, the effect resembles the sound of an experienced orchestra. Conductors determine which music their musicians must play and how to play it. Musicians respond by playing their instruments exactly as directed, interdependently.

Good leadership moves people forward together to accomplish the mission. Leaders should not have to demand anything anymore than orchestra conductors should have to demand that their musicians play exactly what the composer wrote. Conductors simply point the way and serious musicians follow. When leaders become internal to people, directing flows freely and the symphony sounds magnificent.

Having learned the importance of influence and direction for effective leaders, we will now apply those principles to the leadership process. The agenda for the remainder of this chapter includes: 1) The Mission, 2) Technical Formation, 3) Executive Leadership, 4) Mentoring, 5) Supervisory Advice to Leaders, and 6) The Twelve Habits of Effective Leaders.

THE MISSION

Leaders successfully influence and direct people to focus on the mission. In professional spheres of influence, the goal is to fulfill the mission of the organization. In personal spheres of influence, the goal is to fulfill the mission of the individual. It is important for people to write mission statements about the primary focus of their own lives as well as of their organizations. Everything they do, personally or corporately, should revolve around those goals.

Here are some mission statement samples:

The corporate mission statement for the National Aeronautical and Space Administration is this:

> To advance and communicate scientific knowledge and understanding of the earth, the solar system, and the universe. To advance human exploration, use, and development of space. To research, develop, verify, and transfer advanced aeronautics and space technologies.

For individuals, a mission statement would encompass personal ambition. Sandra Preston, a teacher, has this as her mission statement:

> To develop teaching skills in order to enhance others' potential in life.

Ordering all events and schedules around these mission statements results in success.

Everyone is a leader in some areas. Most effective leaders have mission statements at work and at home to help them focus and accomplish their dreams and goals. Readers should feel free to copy the mission statement forms in the appendices, fill them out, and routinely Plan, Implement and Evaluate (PIE) the results. They should repeat this cycle frequently and help others do the same. The primary responsibility of leaders is to empower others to figure out and carry out their mission statements successfully. Being a leader among family, friends, or workers carries a price tag. It means taking responsibility for others through servanthood.

TECHNICAL FORMATION

People at any level are effective leaders if they do their jobs in an outstanding manner. But they must take personal responsibility to go through the technical formation process. Technical formation is mastering one's field of work. It is the process of developing technical proficiency through leadership training. It encompasses a myriad of processes developing technical competence and teamwork.

Technical formation means that a leader is to be a person of character and values, is disciplined, compassionate, a role model, a person of initiative, flexible, consistent, and able to resolve ethical dilemmas.

Leaders not only require much knowledge about their own organizations and other similar types of organizations, but also an understanding of themselves and others, and the ability to know how to work with people at all levels in organizations. Specifically, they must know standards and how those standards affect inner struggles; they must know skills and attitudes. They must know themselves and their inner strengths and weaknesses. Leaders should build on strengths and build up weaknesses to acceptable levels of strength. Leaders should know their people, along with their people's capabilities and limits.

Leaders must do many things well, primarily because they are ultimately responsible for the success of their organizations. Specifically, they must provide people with a purpose, and they must be able to explain the mission to others, such as who, what, where, when, and how. Leaders must equip workers to achieve the organization's mission, including planning and communicating effectively, displaying technical competence, developing subordinates, and setting goals for workers.

Leaders should provide direction for the people under them, and that direction should include:

- Planning and maintaining ethical standards.
- Making good decisions the team accepts.

Moral Leadership

- Solving technical and logistical problems.
- Supervising and evaluating tasks.
- Teaching people what to do.
- Enabling their self-expression.
- Coaching and counseling personnel.
- Training individuals and teams.

Leaders must provide motivation, which includes:

- Serving as a standard-bearer.
- Developing cohesive teams
- Making professional development meaningful.
- Applauding milestones.
- Counseling personnel who fall short of standards.
- Taking care of workers' spiritual needs by encouraging them to seek out spiritual leaders or hiring a corporate chaplain.

Leaders should use the scientific method to make effective decisions. The steps of effective decision-making are these:

1. Interpret the situation.
2. Analyze all factors and applicable forces.
3. Choose the best envisioned course of action.
4. Analyze the results.
5. Re-evaluate and start the process over.

The following principles of job leadership will greatly assist in the technical formation at every level.

THE TWELVE PRINCIPLES OF JOB LEADERSHIP

These principles of leadership provide a foundation for success. We cannot guarantee your next promotion or pay raise, nor can we be certain that unforeseen circumstances may not create a

Effectiveness of the Moral Leader

stumbling block in your journey to the top. But we do guarantee that if you master these time-tested leadership principles, you will be best equipped to face the challenges ahead of you. No one can travel your road as well as you can. You are your own best friend on your particular journey. These are the tools that will help you succeed as a leader.

1. Know yourself and seek self-improvement. Assess your influence on people. Watch for results, listen to feedback, and seek counseling.
2. Be technically proficient. Know and experience what your people go through.
3. Be tactically proficient. Know how to relate to other people and their job fields.
4. Develop skills for the mission—on the job experience. Implement knowledge.
5. Seek and take responsibility. Make sound and timely decisions. Be prepared to make quick decisions.
6. Model desired behavior and character.
7. Know your people. Look out for their well being; otherwise, they will not follow and morale will be low.
8. Keep others informed—leaders, staff, mentors, employees, and volunteers.
9. Develop a sense of responsibility in people. Delegate and give expectations, parameters, deadlines, and tools. Let people decide how to do the best job they can do.
10. Ensure the mission is understood, supervised, and accomplished. Supervise not too much and not too little. The degree of supervision depends on people's skills. Explore the knowledge level and provide training accordingly.
11. Build up the team. Work as a unit. When people trust both you and your staff, there is teamwork.

12. Employ people in accordance with their capabilities. More training equals more capabilities.

EXECUTIVE LEADERSHIP

The role of executive leadership is to develop character and apply leadership principles through various methods. In dealing with organizational situations, the role of executive leadership is to attain teamwork in the team and accomplish the mission.

Leaders guide people through the technical formation process as outlined in company regulations, policies, by-laws, or manuals. They provide feedback on subordinates' professional development. They use discretion on how much personal information to share to maintain professional relationships.

Executive leaders will model outstanding leadership traits and implement leadership development processes. They should have character and embody altruistic behaviors and attitudes. Leaders build bridges to their people to facilitate teamwork. Since people are confined to the limitations of individual levels of expertise, leaders should help each one individually and collectively to be resourceful. Leaders should provide extra training to expand the limits of their followers, and should give direction to help them fulfill their career goals and personal mission statements. In order to help followers fulfill their individual goals, executive leaders should guide subordinates in writing personal mission statements in staff development workshops and retreats.

Senior leaders expect the brightest trainees to rise to the top and watch to see who will step forward to accomplish the necessary tasks. No one should feel intimidated for seeking the guidance of superiors, because it is expected that leaders will mentor subordinates.

MENTORING

Wise leaders seek out senior mentors. Mentors are not mere career counselors, although career counseling is certainly part of mentoring. Mentoring is the one-on-one process of leadership development. In dealing with their spheres of influence, mentors try to develop character, in themselves as well as in others, by applying leadership principles through various methods. A mentor's goal is to help every client attain personal and professional growth so they can accomplish their specific missions.

Mentors guide clients through the leadership development processes, provide feedback on the clients' journeys, and divulge personal struggles through which they have personally traveled in arriving at their current plateau in life. Mentoring requires relationships of trust and confession on the part of both mentors and their clients.

Mentors model leadership traits, build relationship dynamics with their clients, and assess each client's professional development. Mentors provide training and give feedback on leadership skills, stress management, communication skills, and personal growth. They also guide clients in fulfilling mission statements. Mentoring includes inspiration, collegiality, confidence, consultation, and support, while providing a safe atmosphere for sharing problems and successes. Consequently, mentors are instrumental in fostering clients' character formation.

Mentors must have developed their own character traits, embodying altruistic behaviors and attitudes. Mentors may lead clients no further than their own progress. So those who would succeed as leaders should select their mentors carefully. Likewise, mentors might be of no value to those who do not take mentoring seriously. Mentors should ensure that potential clients are ready to grow before assuming mentor-client relationships. They should use personal mission statements as tools in guiding their clients at all levels of leadership.

Moral Leadership

SUPERVISORY ADVICE TO LEADERS

Leaders must be tough in order to get the job done and handle conflict as it arises. Toughness does not preclude being warm-hearted and relational. Supervisory leadership means getting out from behind the desk and personally seeing what is going on. Involvement makes leaders aware of conflict and enables them to resolve problems before they get out of hand. But the key to conflict resolution is being sensitive and listening to people. Involvement enables leaders to determine the make-or-break activities in their organizations.

Conflict may fester in environments where leaders take it for granted that everything is fine. But astute leaders never make this assumption, and when they find conflict, they handle it firmly to resolve it. Leaders should pre-empt divisiveness. Alibis are not helpful and are the leaders' greatest enemies during these times. However, honesty and forthright attempts at mending division can be the leaders' greatest assets.

Challenges to leadership are tremendous, but the rewards of overcoming those challenges are vastly superior to the challenges themselves. Facing all challenges head on will greatly impact leaders' abilities to lead. These opportunities for growth will certainly position leaders for greater successes down the road.

Below are "The Twelve Habits of Effective Leaders." These traits not only facilitate effective leadership but also will inspire onlookers to take note of leaders who emulate these habits.

THE TWELVE HABITS OF EFFECTIVE LEADERS

Bearing

Creating a favorable impression in appearance and personal conduct at all times.

Making a favorable impression does not depend on or result from parading beautiful clothing, making sure others realize you are in a position of authority, or snapping commands. It does include dressing appropriately for the position rather than flaunting expensive, though inappropriate, styles and name-brands. It does include posture, smiling, a demeanor of acceptance, and above all, allowing others to see that the leader thinks everyone in the group or organization is equally important. Followers do not appreciate pride or excessive humility; rather, they appreciate a leader who values them as part of the organization, as someone valuable for contributing to the whole.

Commitment

Pledging in good faith one's determination to work with another.

Cynicism is the sign of our times. There is nothing wrong with healthy skepticism, but when it turns into cynicism, trust in humanity is gone. In the early days of our country, people admired leaders and expected them to hold high standards. Then came the trend to sneer at leaders with high moral standards as "un-cool" or old-fashioned and unrealistic. National leaders are now subject to all kinds of criticism. And often they deserve it. Maybe we were shocked at how immoral some presidents could be, but we should have been even more shocked at how many people took the facts in stride—that leaders' immorality was not a major deterrent to them in their voting patterns. Given that fact, however, we must also admit that if the standard of great leadership is perfection, no one would be a great leader because not one of us is perfect.

Consequently, many leaders today hesitate to use terms such as "morality," "integrity," "selflessness" and "respect." Another of these so-called old-fashioned terms is "commitment." Yet effective leadership always requires commitment. Abraham Lincoln was a master of tactical wheeling and dealing, but he always did so in the context of his commitment to his own principle—to preserve the Union and to live according to the Declaration of Independence.[1] Many corporate leaders have never deviated from their

---

1. O'Toole, *Leadership A to Z*, 41.

commitment to their values, principles, and philosophies of leadership. Although many leaders have not wavered even under pressure from Wall Street and from boards of directors, perhaps the toughest leader of recent years has been former Prime Minister Margaret Thatcher of Great Britain. On the question of commitment, she was adamant: "One changes one's tactics, strategies, and programs as circumstances dictate; but change one's principles? Never."[2]

It is difficult for people to commit to anything (whether company, group, or another person) that they do not understand. Therefore, vague definitions or ambiguous concepts make it almost impossible to attain commitment. The purposes and values of a company or a group must be clearly articulated and consistently enforced if followers will commit to them. Commitment, then, becomes an issue of knowledge, specifically of believable goals, vision, and actions. If a company does not know where it is going, it is very difficult to get a team to go with it.

Decisiveness

Being willing to act and accept responsibility for actions.

What the leader says, the leader must do. Probably nothing is more apt to destroy a leader's position than the inability to make sound decisions and then to stay with or act on those decisions. While all leaders need to hear the opinions of others involved, the leaders are the ones to make the decisions, so never should those leaders ask others what should be done. After evaluating all the data, the leader makes the best decision for the good of the whole company, group, or business. Most followers have their own areas of interest, so they see specifically from a certain viewpoint. The leader is required to see the global opportunities and problems from the position of the whole; this enables him to make more informed decisions that will impact and benefit the whole group. The leader

---

2. Ibid., 42.

is therefore able to get to the heart of complex issues and to see both the negative and positive possibilities.

Dependability

Being totally reliable in attitude, word and action at all times.

Leadership is the principle of exerting influence within a group so that the group can move toward accomplishing its goals of performance and permanence. Leaders should constantly monitor their own performance so that they can achieve the level of dependability they expect from their followers. Dependability applies to actions, of course, but also to words. When leaders speak, others need to know that those words will be carried out—that they are more than just words but are accompanied by the intentions that will show they are actions as well. The manners, words, and actions of leaders must be totally reliable at all times. Trust from followers depends on the reliability of the leader.

Endurance

Withstanding, with mental and physical stamina, any fatigue, distress, and hardship associated with leading.

Difficulties do exist. Leaders will have problems and get discouraged. However, endurance will remind a leader that every problem has a solution. Endurance means not giving up when difficulties surface. When leaders question whether they should quit, or give up, they need to remember their vision. If they will focus on their goals and visualize those goals as already accomplished (or almost accomplished), they will be able to renew their commitment and stay with the job until it is completed. Many of the world's greatest leaders found great difficulty in carrying out their visions, but they were successful because of their endurance. They endured to the end so that the success could be seen.

Energy

Acting as the catalyst implemented to effect change.

Most leaders do not do the actual work of change or organizational decision-making. So what do leaders do? A leader is much like the conductor of a symphony orchestra. The conductor is in front of the orchestra doing his arm-waving job. But most of the instrumentalists are not looking at the conductor—they are looking at the music. What, then, is the purpose of a conductor? He gets the musicians working together before the performance. He energizes the orchestra to want to sound their best. In the same way, a corporate leader energizes the company or organization, making the team members want to work together so that they can produce the most harmonious results possible. Leaders energize organizations by sharing their own natural enthusiasm and by sharing their convictions about what should be and could be if everyone got together and produced the best results.

James O'Toole compares the energy of a corporate leader to that of a cheerleader. He says the natural action of any group tends to go toward flatness or just getting by. The job of a leader is to get the group moving, to get them to do something and to enjoy doing it at the same time.[3] The energy must be authentic and not hidden so that it will be contagious.

Integrity

Being upright in character and willing to abide by moral principles; absolute truthfulness.

Integrity may seem to be an old-fashioned trait left over from the Boy Scouts. However, it is more than a word or a left-over idea from the past. Integtiry is the key to effective leadership because it suggests wholeness, rightness, and a sense of moral soundness. Included in the concept of integrity would be personal beliefs and values, organizational aims, and individual behavior. It is not

---

3. Ibid., 94.

limited to right and wrong actions, but it encompasses all of a leader's process of leading.

Integrity is a daily quest for consistency in one's personal beliefs, consistency in one's vision for an organization, and consistency in one's behavior. Badaracco and Ellsworth conducted a survey to determine the most desired personal traits in a leader. The responses they received revealed three dominating traits: a strong set of personal ethical standards (especially honesty and fairness, which are the basis for trust and loyalty), a positive belief in others (in the latent ability of other people), and a strong, compelling vision for their companies.[4] During the survey, another idea surfaced with strong conviction: a desire that high ethical standards or values pervade the company. The "most commonly mentioned values were honesty, fairness, mutual respect and trust, compassion, and sensitivity in the exercise of power."[5] Findings of this nature remind us how important integrity really is to those who follow. No one wants to be deceived by a leader.

Judgment

Weighing facts and possible solutions as a base for making sound decisions affecting others.

Much of the training to be a leader comes from the classroom of life. Leaders learn by trial and error, by making mistakes and resolving those errors. As the learning takes place, judgment increases. The immature judgments of non-experience change into the mature judgments of experience and knowledge. Knowledge and judgment go together because the more leaders know about the business and people under their leadership, the better they can use proper judgment in making decisions regarding those people and that business. The need for judging skills is apparent for a leader. We define ourselves by the judgments we make and by the moral stance upheld by those judgments.

---

4. Badaracco and Ellsworth, *Leadership and Quest for Integrity*, 99–101.
5. Ibid., 104.

Knowledge

Acquiring information and understanding people.

Knowledge is such a large area of leadership because it covers so many aspects of a leader's life. A legitimate question might be "What kind of knowledge?" Necessary areas of knowledge might include social skills, ethics, interpersonal skills, communication skills, writing skills, complex reasoning skills, industry knowledge, market knowledge, and competitive knowledge. Added to those would be the people skills necessary to relate to followers. Knowledge is essential, of course, in all of these areas, even though we realize that no one can know everything. However, a leader will also often need to operate by instinct. When a leader has all the knowledge available for an area of decision and still does not have a clear answer to all the questions or concerns, that leader may need to depend on knowledge plus instincts to get the best possible solution.

Loyalty

Adhering faithfully to one's God, family, country, and others.

Loyalty is not something a boss or leader can demand. It is something the constituency gives to those who have earned it. Loyalty comes when the followers decide that the organization and its leaders are capable of meeting their needs. Loyal customers are won when they judge the company capable of solving their problems and meeting their needs. This judgment by the followers may be conscious or subconscious, but it must come as a result of their perception that the leader or organization has a solution congruent with their inner needs or problems. True loyalty goes beyond allegiance to one single person as a leader. In fact, we can agree that "When a values-driven leader's actions are successful in institutionalizing values in a company, the organization becomes the focus of loyalty instead of the leader."[6]

---

6. Ibid., 90.

Selflessness

Sacrificing personal desires or requirements for the benefit of others.

Leadership is creativity and self-expression, but it is also servanthood. A leader needs to be a good follower before he can be a good leader. One of the most important roles of leaders is to help people believe in themselves and in their ability to be effective and influential, and to believe that their goals are possible and that there is a better future that they can move toward through their own efforts. Leaders must put others first. Their followers' goals, needs, and futures must be at least as important, and maybe even more important, than their own goals, needs, and futures. That is selfless leading.

Tact

Leading others effectively without creating offense.

Leaders are usually optimists and believers in hope. Often the followers become discouraged or depressed because they do not see the kind of progress, or the speed of progress, they desire. Perhaps they do not see because their view is limited to one unit of the organization. But whatever the reason, it happens. It is the job of the leaders to keep morale up and to keep hope and inspiration alive in the business. Moral leaders will always treat each person under their leadership as special and worthwhile. Tact requires equal treatment for all workers and followers. Beyond that, however, a sense of humanity itself requires that leaders believe all workers are of equal value. When leaders believe that, the loyalty and efficiency of the workers will increase, because they will respond to that belief.

These twelve habits sum up what followers expect of leaders. We want our leaders to be inspiring and enthusiastic about the future. We expect them to be able to communicate a vision for the future that we can accept and help accomplish. Enthusiasm and excitement are essential. However, the single most important ingredient in the relationship between leader and constituent is honesty. All followers want to know that the person they follow is truthful, ethical, and principled. We want a leader's behavior to be consistent with the words spoken. In fact, we usually judge someone as honest if we observe a consistency between that person's words and actions. We expect our leaders to model the ethics and values we admire. When we see that kind of modeling and consistency in our leaders, we believe them to be honest, and we will follow them into their vision for the future.

five

Core Values for Moral Leadership

MORAL LAWS ARE UNIVERSAL because they are actually fundamental human values, such as truth, goodness, beauty, courage, and justice. The experience of pursuing values such as truth and goodness is considered a moral experience. Mortimer Adler went even further when he said that when we are thinking of truth, goodness, and beauty, we are thinking of values. In fact, he stated that the values underlying truth, goodness, and beauty become the means by which we judge our own behavior.[1]

Such values are essential for development of character, and must be incorporated into our behavior. Specifically, Clarence Walton observes that "Character is more than what simply happens to people. It is what they do to themselves." Humans shape their own characters. We constantly choose between right and wrong. Each decision a person makes shapes a person and the future behavior of that person.[2] Norman Schwarzkopf, Former Commander, U. S. Central Command, states, "Leadership involves conduct, and conduct is determined by values. These values [may

---

1. Adler, *Six Great Ideas*, 24.
2. Walton, *Moral Managers*, 7, 176.

Moral Leadership

be called] by many names—ethics, morality, and integrity come to mind.... Values are what make us who we are."[3]

Core values, then, clearly and definitely determine who we are. They are not just what we do, but they define what and who we are as human beings. We emulate the values we choose to follow because they are the standard for our behavior, not only in our homes, our work places, or our churches, but in any ordered society. Sadly, some people are confused about values because they have never been taught the difference between right and wrong. Values demand that we do not just get by every day the best way we can and get away with whatever we can, but that we determine what our actions will be and what our code of behavior will be.

Core values in the military are personal character qualities that are corporately recognized as essential to the life of an organization. They unite, motivate, and guide an organization in its mission. And they unite the people involved in that organization so that all will work together for the same goals.

In fact, values training is incorporated into every basic training unit for the U. S. military.[4] There are seven separate values taught throughout basic training, in blocks of instruction on core values. Privates must not only know the values, but also be able to recite the definitions and explain real life examples of appropriate actions and behavior demonstrating each value. Knowledge and understanding of Army values is mandatory for graduation from basic training. The Army defines its core values as follows:

- Loyalty—Bear true faith and allegiance to the U. S. Constitution, the Army, and other soldiers.
- Duty—Fulfill your obligations.
- Respect—Treat people as they should be treated.
- Selfless Service—Put the welfare of the nation, the Army, and your subordinates before your own.
- Honor—Live up to all the Army values.

3. Schwarzkopf, *Ethical Leadership*, 2.
4. Army Core Values, 1.

- Integrity—Do what is right, legally and morally.
- Personal Courage—Face fear, danger, or adversity (physically and morally).

These values form the acronym LDRSHIP—an interesting parallel because these values are truly essential for anyone who would be a leader. These core values are esteemed moral attributes based on unchanging principles of life. Leaders would do well to adapt and apply them or use them as a basis for selecting values more fitting to their own areas of leadership.

General Douglas MacArthur delivered a speech at the U. S. Military Academy (USMA) at West Point, New York, on May 12, 1962. It was reprinted forty years later in observance of Memorial Day. In the speech, MacArthur said that many people look at terms such as "duty," honor" and "country" as simply words. However, they are not mere words, MacArthur asserted, for they are much more: "They build your basic character. They mold you for your future roles . . . They make you strong enough to know when you are weak . . . They teach you not to substitute words for action . . . to learn to stand up in the storm, and to have compassion on those who fall; to master yourself before you seek to master others; to have a heart that is clean, a goal that is high."[5] These are the kinds of value traits that should be evident in all good leaders.

Pulitzer Prize winner James MacGregor Burns, in his book *Leadership*, stresses the moral character of leadership. He distinguishes values-driven leadership—which he calls "transforming" leadership—from "transactional" leadership (leaders exchange money, power, and perks for the actions they want their followers to take). Burns writes, "Transforming leadership ultimately becomes moral in that it raises the level of human conduct and ethical aspirations of both leader and led, and thus it has a transforming effect on both."[6]

For leadership to be successful, it is essential that one delineate the necessary qualities, characteristics, and approaches

5. MacArthur, *Washington Times*, 2002.
6. Burns, *Leadership*, 20.

for leadership of each specific environment. Some people project the future directions of our country and world, specifying which leadership styles may be relevant for future businesses and governments. However, forecasting techniques will always have limits; we cannot be certain what the future will bring.

Alfred Decrane, however, suggests that there is one model that can help us put some meaningful concepts into leadership in business. He calls it the "constitutional model" because James Madison and other framers of the U. S. Constitution "constructed a document embodying certain core principles to guide the lives of the American people and to establish the framework of governance."[7] These framers constructed a document that had to be worded broadly enough to be effective for many specific daily issues as well as for changing conditions and for future challenges they could not envision. Many years later, in the twenty-first century, we still see that the fundamental principles guiding the Constitution continue to survive, regardless of the huge number of amendments and attempts to interpret them in ways amenable to specific contemporary purposes.

In the same way, core qualities of leadership can be identified, even though they may need to be qualified and modified and reapplied as conditions change and new challenges arise. The truly basic qualities remain solid and relevant.[8] Those core qualities of leadership would include (in addition to basic leadership skills) character, vision, behavior, and confidence. These traits endure despite all social, political, and business changes. These basic leadership principles help individuals at all stages of responsibility to lead and to model what a leader should be. The constitutional model suggests that leaders will adapt these core competencies to the challenges of their time and the areas of their responsibilities.

An important job of leaders is to build self-confidence in their followers. The followers often need to be convinced that they are, in fact, more capable than they give themselves credit for being. And if the leader says, "Come on, we can do it!" that is even

7. Decrane, *Leaders of the Future*, 250.
8. Ibid.

Core Values for Moral Leadership

more significant because of the "we." Working together is much more effective than working alone. If *we* are in this together, *we* can help each other. The leader starts this process by building a safety net to catch followers when they fall or fail. Failure is not the end. Rather, it is an opportunity to try again, to change something that did not work. Effective leaders will be sure their followers realize this important fact.

Participatory leading will not lead to perfection or utopian business deals. However, it will result in everyone working together. Not everyone in the group will agree about everything, but working in harmony gives everyone a chance to contribute. It makes followers feel respected. Leaders can turn resisters into followers by simply including them in the process of change. When leaders respect followers, the followers will respect leaders.

Long-time coach and teacher John Wooden prepared a "Pyramid of Success" in which he not only listed but placed in a triangle (pyramid) the traits he considered essential for succeeding in life (see Figure 1 for my revision of Wooden's diagram).

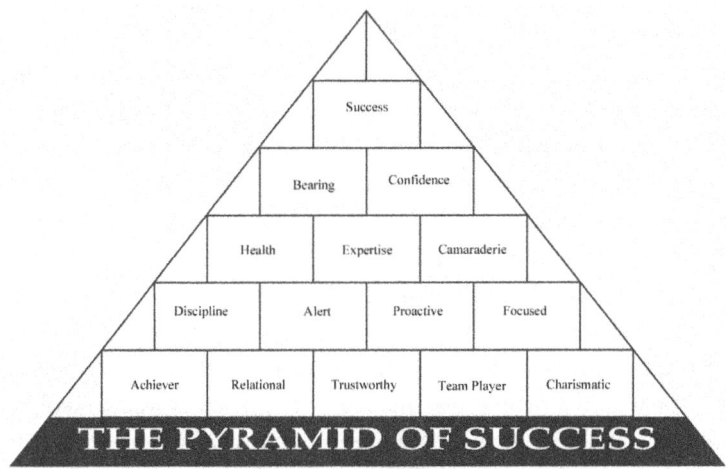

Figure 1. Pyramid of Success

Listing these traits shows how they build upon each other: enthusiasm, cooperation, loyalty, friendship, industriousness,

Moral Leadership

intentness, initiative, alertness, self-control, team spirit, skill, condition, poise, confidence, and competitive greatness. Notice that the one most athletes might think most significant, competitive greatness, stands upon the foundation of earlier values in character, such as loyalty, cooperation, and friendship. To complete the triangle, Wooden places other traits along the two sides to hold the previously listed traits together. He includes adaptability, resourcefulness, faith, patience, integrity, reliability, and honesty among those that hold the other skills together.[9] Again, notice that Wooden emphasizes the values and character traits, stressing them as components to success. To succeed, we must work on those parts of our character that stress values.

As long as we are human, we will grow and develop, and thus we will require change, a constant "being in process." Our leadership skills will grow at the same time growth is improving our characters. Leadership requires growth since people are not born with leadership skills in place.

Most companies talk about the "value added" components of organizational production. Such a term usually has to do with the relationship of all major factors involved in production (i.e., money, materials, people, overhead, etc.). However, for a moral leader the value added is not simply the formula for profit or the increased productivity of goods. Instead, it is increased trust in, and from, the human beings involved in the organization. Such trust comes from the value that the leadership places on the respect, loyalty, honor, integrity, and service due those involved in that production. In other words, such values—demonstrated both in the leaders' own characters and toward all individuals involved in the company—will be the difference between a profit-oriented company and a people-oriented company. Such "value added" relates specifically to the people of the group, for those people demonstrate the values the organization esteems.

A moral leader, or one who intends to be moral, has a model in Scripture. The Apostle Peter gives us the qualifications for moral leaders. He tells us that leaders are to care for others with diligence,

9. Hill and Wooden, *Be Quick*, 10–11.

not because they have to but because they want to, not calculating what they can get out of it, but acting spontaneously, not telling others what to do (not being bossy), but showing the way (being a model or a pattern of the way). Leaders are to be down to earth with followers (pride goes before a fall), to inspire others to follow, not to put on airs, and to stay alert. This is certainly great advice for any leader.[10]

The same writer, the Apostle Peter, gives the traits of poor (non-moral) leaders: Poor leaders lie, they will say anything that sounds good to exploit followers, and they encourage destructive divisions. They pit one person against another, and when they fail they will take everyone with them. They can't tell right from wrong, they are out for themselves only, they live by lust, and they indulge in self-rule egotism. In addition (as if that were not enough), they despise interference from any true authority above them, speak evil of other leaders and authority figures, are addicted to pleasure, and are greedy.[11]

What a negative picture of a leader. Yet some so-called leaders fit the description—"so-called" because true leaders would not try to lead that way. How much better to be the kind of leader described in the first definition! Our values will determine the kind of leader we will be. A good leader will be able to say with Gideon, "Look at me and do likewise . . . Behold . . . do as I do."[12]

A good leader is a moral model of personhood as well as of leadership.

---

10. I Peter 5.
11. II Peter 2.
12. Judges 7:17, KJV 2011.

six

Team Leadership

PEOPLE WANT TEAMWORK. THEY want to know that somebody—senior leader, CEO, supervisor, mentor, teacher, rabbi, pastor, or loved one—wants them on the team and will facilitate bonding. In any sphere of influence, there are ways to develop teamwork. Effective team leadership includes ethical decision-making, core values, empowering, enabling, change, communication and feedback, relationship building, leadership improvement methods, and conflict resolution. So let's analyze these processes.

DECISION-MAKING TECHNIQUES

A central skill for leaders is decision-making. Whether or not the leaders always make decisions themselves, they will need to be able to help others on their teams make the best decisions and ensure that they are accepted by the whole team.

There are four primary decision-making techniques: voting, consensus, unilateral decision-making, and decision matrices. Voting, consensus, and matrices require others' input. Unilateral decisions exclude input unless leaders consciously solicit it. Being allowed to give input enhances people's moral support and empowers them to own the process. When leaders communicate issues clearly, they enable people to support them. Clear communication also conveys the leaders' concerns about how their decisions impact those involved.

Matrices are unique. Leaders use matrices for quantitative approaches. Matrices can prevent unwise decisions and the consequential result of wasted resources—money, manpower, training, and time. Delegating an individual or a small team of two or three individuals to use matrices to recommend a course of action (COA) may be the smartest way to invite input and to save resources. Let's examine each decision-making technique.

Voting

Voting is the decision-making process used to determine the will of the majority of a given populace. Voting is the most common way to make decisions. When there is no time or too many people involved so that it is almost impossible to reach a consensus, voting is the next best option. It is a more efficient method of group decision-making. But because it is a win/lose solution, voting may result in division and hard feelings. Those members on the losing side may have interests and rights at risk, all of which may need protection with rules and regulations.

Consensus

Consensus is the unanimous agreement of the people. This method is most ideal. Consensus empowers everyone to have a voice in decision-making. Again, it is not efficient when time constraints are a factor.

Consensus is a win/win method benefiting everyone. It requires everyone to discuss issues until they all agree. It means that all concerned have no reservations so strong that they cannot support one common goal. They are all committed to the same course of action. The leader's role is facilitating the discussion to produce a consensus. This role prevents leaders from either concurring or nonconcurring on issues. Otherwise, if leaders get involved in supporting one side over the other, they can sway the majority's perspective, defeat the purpose, and cause the minority to feel betrayed.

In the consensus process, the leader 1) states the purpose of the discussion and presents the problem, 2) states possible solutions and asks the group to discuss them, and 3) asks members to voice their opinions one at a time. If there is a consensus, the leader proceeds to the next item on the agenda and repeats the process. Otherwise, if there is no consensus, the leader identifies what can and cannot be agreed on, states the alternatives, and repeats the process until the group reaches a consensus. Below are guidelines for a consensus. Careful attention to this guide will facilitate reaching a consensus.

Seven Guidelines for a Consensus

1. Understand others before explaining your view.
2. Present all relevant data.
3. Discuss options thoroughly with all members.
4. Distinguish between problems and symptoms.
5. Beware of easy answers.
6. Avoid competition.
7. Choose the best course of action.

Consensus may be the healthiest way of making community decisions, but a consensus may not be possible in radically different groups, or about subjects such as politics, because there is such a disparity of opinion. However, some compromise and some effort or attempt to reason something of value in another's view is part of consensus. Strong feelings should never overcome reason. The search for reason and truth should eventually bring the team to an acceptable compromise.

Unilateral Decisions

Sometimes leaders make unilateral decisions they deem best. They usually do so under one of three conditions:

1. Issues are too far above subordinates' levels of expertise.
2. Consensus is not possible.
3. Deadlines prevent voting.

The danger of such decision-making is obvious—when leaders make unilateral decisions, not all subordinates will be as emotionally committed to the decision since they were not allowed to own the process or to give input. The more people are permitted to own the process, the more emotionally and mentally committed they are to the decisions. The levels of commitment to the various decision-making techniques are as follows:

- Unilateral (Low Commitment)
- Voting (Moderate Commitment)
- Decision Matrix (Moderate/High Commitment)
- Consensus (High Commitment)

Ten Team Building Rules

Leaders might post these ten team building rules on the wall or write them on a dry erase board to build teamwork during group discussions and decision-making processes.

1. Respect others.
2. Take responsibility for leading.
3. Listen before speaking.
4. If you have questions, ask them.
5. Don't criticize anything or anyone.
6. Be open-minded.

Moral Leadership

7. Consider every idea equally important.
8. Share experiences, feelings and concerns.
9. Commit to building relationships.
10. Share humor.

Closely connected to these ten rules, but different, of course, because each leader's view shows a different perspective, would be Robert Dale's "Team Building's Ten Commandments."[1] Dale's perspective comes from church organizations; nevertheless, he offers some helpful advice for anyone leading a team of any kind. Here are his ten:

1. Develop personal ownership of your team's life and work. People support what they help create. Anyone who feels important in a group will contribute.
2. Surface expectations. Everyone expects something from the groups they take part in. It takes common concerns to get people to work together.
3. Create a "we" climate. People like to have a sense of kinship, of being drawn together. A "we" atmosphere occurs when leaders take responsibility for failures and share successes.
4. Recognize relational roles in teams. A broad range of relational roles and abilities will exist in any group. You must take care of the diversity of people and roles.
5. Do team repair. Groups need maintenance in order to run smoothly.
6. Define the core mission of the organization. No team will function effectively without a clear vision of its task.
7. Identify the formal task groups you work with. Organize any overlap of responsibilities. Be aware of different roles each person is called upon to provide in different groups.

---

1. Dale, *Ministers as Leaders*, 100–104.

8. Develop team task descriptions. Task descriptions cut down on gaps and overlaps in production. Teams work more effectively when they are certain of tasks.
9. Monitor task roles on your team. Several roles for one person or too many overlapping roles can keep a team from progressing as it should.
10. Learn to manage meetings. Guiding a process in meetings is better than controlling people. The key is to balance relationships and tasks in work teams.

The Decision Matrix

Matrices are the friend of the systematic leader. Anyone who likes to be objective can relate to a tool that allows a decision maker to evaluate different courses of action in an objective and systematic manner. The first step in making a decision matrix is to create a raw data matrix. Along one side of the matrix (down the left-hand side) list each course of action (COA) being considered. Along the intersecting side (across the top of the matrix) list any and all options that will be used as part of the comparison to determine the courses of action. Please see Figure 2 for an example of a raw data matrix for a decision to purchase a car.

Criteria / COA	miles per gallon	cost	warranty term
Car 1	20	17K	48 months
Car 2	25	20K	60 months
Car 3	30	25K	36 months

Figure 2. Raw Data Matrix

As we examine the raw data that show up on the graph, we can evaluate and compare the possible courses of action. It is absolutely essential to be sure that the raw data or the basic information is accurate, or the evaluation and comparison will not be dependable.

The simplest matrix involves assigning relative values to each criterion (rank ordering the courses of action). Please see the unweighted relative values matrix in Figure 3. For example, in the raw data matrix (Figure 2), Car 3 has the best miles per gallon (MPG) or a relative value of 1, Car 2 has the second best MPG or a relative value of 2, and Car 1 has the worst MPG or a relative value of 3.

Criteria / COA	miles per gallon	cost	warranty term	Total
Car 1	3	1	2	6
Car 2	2	2	1	5
Car 3	1	3	3	7

Figure 3. Relative Values Matrix (unweighted)

By looking carefully at the criteria values for each course of action, we can see that Car 2 has the best total score among the three. However, because some information may be more significant when the decision is to be made, at least to the one doing the evaluating, we may want to use a more sophisticated matrix with a technique known as weighting. This technique is important in many decisions when it becomes necessary to stipulate more weight or significance to some criteria than to others. In the preceding example, if cost happened to be significantly more important in the decision than either miles per gallon or warranty term, we could assign it a weight of three and thereby increase its relevance in the weighted relative values matrix in Figure 4 below.

Notice that the cost criteria values for the three courses of action are now 3, 6, and 9 instead of 1, 2, and 3. Each unweighted relative value was multiplied by the weighting factor of three to arrive at the weighted values in the matrix. Notice how the weighting process changed the results. After weighting the cost of the

Team Leadership

car, Car 1 is now the best course of action in the matrix due to the significance of cost in the decision process.

Criteria / COA	miles per gallon weight=1	cost weight=3	warranty term weight =1	Total less is best
Car 1	3	3 (1x3)	2	8
Car 2	2	6 (2x3)	1	9
Car 3	1	9 (3x3)	3	13

Figure 4. Relative Values Matrix (weighted)

For even more significant decisions, there may be a need for a more sophisticated matrix. The most sophisticated form of a decision matrix involves using a multiplication process instead of relative values to evaluate each course of action. In this case, you would multiply the criteria raw data in order to arrive at a total matrix score. Since not every criterion is best when less (i.e., miles per gallon and warranty term are best when more), the mathematical inverse of "best when more" criteria is used in the multiplication process to keep the matrix total score on a consistent less is best basis. Please see the multiplication matrix (unweighted) of the preceding example in Figure 5.

Criteria / COA	miles per gallon	cost	warranty term	Total less is best
Car 1	1/20	17	1/48	.018
Car 2	1/25	20	1/60	.013
Car 3	1/30	25	1/36	.023

Figure 5. Multiplication Matrix (unweighted)

Using a multiplication matrix (unweighted), Car 2 is the best course of action. A multiplication matrix can be weighted in the same manner as a relative values matrix. If cost is a significantly more important factor, and we assign it a weight of three, our multiplication matrix would now look differently. Please see the weighted multiplication matrix in Figure 6.

Criteria \ COA	miles per gallon weight=1	cost weight=3	warranty term weight =1	Total less is best
Car 1	1/20	51 (17x3)	1/48	.053
Car 2	1/25	60 (20x3)	1/60	.040
Car 3	1/30	75 (25x3)	1/36	.069

Figure 6. Multiplication Matrix (weighted)

Unlike the relative values example, the weighting using a multiplication process didn't change the result in this case (COA 2 is still best). This illustrates the differences that can result when using a multiplication matrix versus a relative values matrix. The multiplication matrix is generally considered more accurate. This accuracy is due to the multiplication model taking into account the exact differences between the criteria for each COA, whereas the relative values matrix assigns ranking order values (1, 2, 3, etc.) even in instances where there is very little actual difference between the raw data amounts. For example, cost in the above example differed by only 8K (see Figure 2) among the three courses of action. The relative values matrix (Figure 3) assigns a value of 1 to the best cost COA and 3 to the worst cost COA. Although the actual costs for COA 1 and COA 3 differed by less that 50 percent (Figure 2), the relative values indicated a 300 percent difference (Figure 3).

For many decisions, the decision matrix represents a way to evaluate and compare the various courses of action systematically. In addition to doing the analysis manually, one can purchase decision matrix software commercially.

Ethical Decision-Making

Ethical leaders make ethical decisions. Ethical leaders account for both accidental and purposeful actions and do not make excuses or blame others for the outcomes. When faced with important decisions, ethical leaders *think, choose,* and *act*. Ethical decisions are based on what is right or wrong, and those making such decisions must take into consideration these six factors:

- Beliefs—a body of truths to which one adheres.
- Character—moral excellence and firmness (*Webster*).
- Ethics—a normative standard of moral duty.
- Morals—principles of right and wrong behavior (based on absolutes).
- Principles—unchanging rules of life (permanent as are the laws of nature).
- Values—esteemed moral attributes (for example, the Army Core Values are loyalty, duty, respect, selfless service, honor, integrity, and personal courage—LDRSHIP).

The following questions facilitate ethical decision-making. For each decision, ask these questions:

1. *Is it based on character-based principles?* Effective leaders consistently make decisions based on ethics. Ethics are based on unchanging, time-tested principles of life.
2. *Is it legal?* Ethical leaders make decisions within the framework of the law. Legal issues are significant because there are so many laws affecting organizations, ranging from building codes to copyrights. Laws governing the way we do business continually change.
3. *Is it fair?* Fairness is an issue toward which everyone is sensitive. Fairness considers everyone's interests and rights regarding equality, gender, ethnicity, and equal opportunity. Win/win solutions are usually indicators of fairness, as opposed to win/lose solutions, which usually take advantage of someone.

EMPOWERMENT

Empowerment is giving away authority to individuals to make decisions at their levels of expertise. Empowerment enables people to foster teamwork among their peers, to be resourceful, and to take charge. The skilled use of power is essential to empowerment. Power is the control to effect change.

Giving away authority might intimidate leaders who fear losing power. Rather than being fearful of losing power, however, a leader should realize that giving away authority is giving rights to individuals. Leaders can easily reclaim these rights if people misuse or abuse them. Empowerment may easily intimidate individuals who have not previously been empowered. Empowerment levels should be based on individual capabilities and the gravity of the consequences. Consequently, leaders must assess people's capabilities in the three following areas: 1) training achieved, 2) judgmental ability, and 3) experience.[2]

Successfully empowering individuals facilitates confidence so they can contribute to their organizations' mission accomplishment. Their organizations will increasingly depend on them as they ascend the corporate ladder. A cycle will have been set in motion in which increasing responsibility and an expanding sphere of influence fuel each other. Successful empowerment frees leaders to focus on the overall functioning of the organization and allows people to receive the maximum benefits of on the job training.

The failure of leaders to ascertain individuals' abilities may result in the subordinates' failure. These failures may discourage individuals from ever accepting empowerment again, and they might never venture into any realm of leadership. Moral leaders will try to evaluate carefully and fairly to make the most of each follower's strengths.

Below are Four Stages of Empowerment, a modification of the "Empowerment Model" in the Quality Air Force Leaders Course. This chart enables leaders to ascertain people's abilities.

---

2. Quality Air Force Leaders Course, 2–27.

Please weigh these stages carefully as you match them with your subordinates' capacities to be empowered.

Four Stages of Empowerment

- Stage 1: Not empowered: Do not handle this task at this time.
- Stage 2: Approval: Ask me before doing this task.
- Stage 3: Update: Take on the mission, but update me.
- Stage 4: Totally empowered: Handle it by yourself.

The ideal atmosphere in your surroundings is an empowered environment. To create an empowered setting, envision an empowered environment in your corporation or home. Everyone understands the boundaries, is aligned to the established vision, and realizes that everyone contributes to actualizing that vision. Picture everyone fulfilling his or her proper role to fulfill that mission. Now, ask yourself the following questions:

- How do individuals treat each other?
- How do individuals treat newcomers?
- Do individuals reach out to others?
- How do they communicate with each other?
- Are problems identified?
- How are the problems identified?
- Why are there problems?
- Are the problems solvable?
- How are the problems solved?
- Are there decisions to make?
- How are decisions made?
- Who makes decisions?

- Do people ask for help?
- Who helps those requesting assistance?

Next, identify the gaps between your ideal environment and your real environment. Explore the immediate steps you can take to bridge these gaps. Select the options you believe would best bridge the gaps. And, finally, implement these options over time as your real environment increasingly reflects your envisioned environment.

ENABLING

Enabling is providing the resources to get the job done. Resources consist of money, manpower, training, and time. Without enabling subordinates, organizational leaders and organizations cannot accomplish their missions. Leaders must enable their subordinates to the degree they want the organization to succeed.

Money must be allotted to procure personnel. To function at their optimum levels, personnel must be trained to function in a variety of related fields. Varied training also allows the organization to receive maximum benefits from the manpower. Time must then be allowed to implement this training. Otherwise, the resources that went into training will have been wasted and the overall morale of the people will decrease. Training and implementation of new skills must be a continual improvement effort. Leaders should assist their subordinates in implementing the training provided. Assistance is in keeping with the philosophy that subordinates are leaders' customers and that servanthood, relationships, and teamwork are important.

IMPROVING YOUR SERVE

Leaders are shown to be effective in implementing change to the degree that they serve. Leaders may improve their serve by answering the following questions:

- What specifically are my subordinates' growth areas and needs?
- What assistance will each of my subordinates accept from me?
- To what degree will my subordinates accept my mentoring?
- How can I measure the level of my subordinates' needs with my level of output?
- Do I need to negotiate my level of output with my subordinates?
- Have I counted the cost of meeting my subordinates' needs in light of my own limitations?

Since some leaders find it difficult to find time to serve and assist subordinates in specific growth areas, they may need to delegate responsibility to skilled volunteers. Then the leaders should assign homework to those who need to grow. This homework should be tailored to individual needs. Leaders should then plan follow-up appointments to counsel and train all potential leaders to strengthen any possible weaknesses accordingly. Leaders should pace themselves to avoid burnout.

LEADERSHIP PARADIGMS

The paradigms below illustrate leadership models. The benefit of the Traditional Leadership Paradigm (Figure 7) is that it shows that the authority in any organization rightfully belongs at the top.

Moral Leadership

Figure 7. Traditional Leadership Paradigm

The Traditional Leadership Paradigm shows that subordinates help leaders get their work done so that they fulfill the mission. This paradigm does not adequately illustrate how leaders may effectively empower subordinates. Leaders are encouraged to reverse this model to empower subordinates as shown in the Empowerment Leadership Paradigm below (Figure 8).

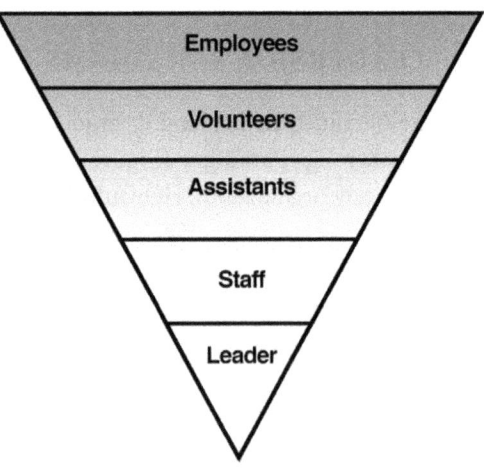

Figure 8. Empowerment Leadership Paradigm

Team Leadership

The Empowerment Leadership Paradigm shows leaders as servants who empower subordinates. Subordinates are dependent on leaders for empowerment and authority. But people viewing this model may get the idea that the leader does not really have the authority. So it can be misleading. Nevertheless, this model means that leaders help subordinates get their work done and that subordinates fulfill the mission. Empowerment improves subordinates' leadership skills, teamwork, productivity, and relationships, and it also reveals the leaders' trust in the expertise of their subordinates. These models are based on concepts from the Quality Air Force Institute.[3]

The third leadership paradigm is the Spherical Leadership Paradigm (Figure 9). The one below is just a sample.

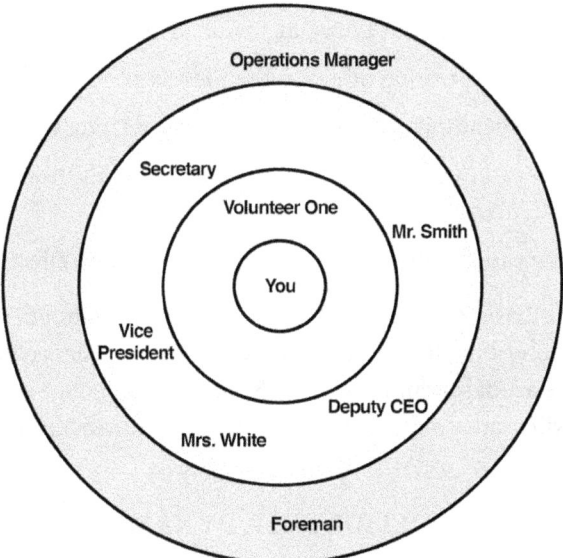

Figure 9. Spherical Leadership Paradigm

Each paradigm circle will obviously differ from person to person. It does not illustrate positions of authority or servanthood as the previous models do. But what it does show is the effectiveness

---

3. Quality Air Force Leaders Course, 1–4.

Moral Leadership

of one's leadership in terms of those being influenced. Leaders and subordinates must draw their own sphere of leadership model with themselves in the center, and they must pinpoint the degree to which they are influencing others in the organization as accurately as possible. They may draw other similar spheres depicting how well they influence family members or friends.

The goal of expanding one's sphere of influence is not to get outsiders into the circle, but to encompass everyone in the organization. Expand those rings. To do so, note the following considerations:

- What measures can I take to influence those outside the sphere?
- What needs do they have?
- What training can I provide to enhance their skills?
- Am I empowering others at their levels of potential?
- Am I spending quality time with those outside the sphere?
- How can I positively affect relationships with those I am not influencing?
- How can I enable others to do their jobs more effectively?

The basis of these considerations is servanthood. Another way of describing it is *customer satisfaction*. As leaders continue to learn the art of servanthood, their spheres of influence in all walks of life will increasingly expand, as will their leadership roles.

RELATIONSHIP DYNAMICS

These leadership models are all about how leaders perceive relationships with subordinates. Relationships consist of interactive processes. Teamwork grows as relationships develop between individuals. The Relationship Dynamics Wheel (Figure 10) below illustrates the elements at work in successful relationships in any sphere of influence. It shows how to make relationships powerful and active. Certainly, relationships may differ in intensity and in the amount of time it takes for them to develop. The Relationship Dynamics Wheel is an enhanced version of the Air Force Office of Special Investigation's (AFOSI) Relationship Model.[4]

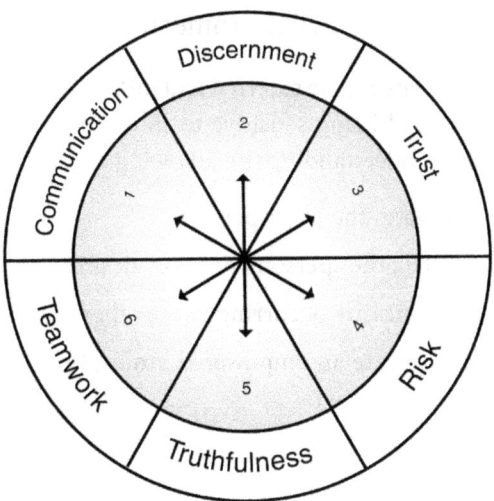

Figure 10. Relationship Dynamics Wheel

This Relationship Dynamics Wheel consists of six steps that will result in teamwork. Teamwork develops as relationships develop between individuals. The following six steps illustrate the elements at work in developing teamwork in any sphere of influence.

1. Communication

Communication is the art of transmitting and receiving messages. Direct the communication toward topics with which the other person feels comfortable. Ask open-ended questions without probing. When areas of common interest have been discovered, direct the communication to personal levels until the conversation is spontaneous and free flowing. Those who remain engaged

---

4. Air Force, *Quality Team Training*, 18.

in communication have a better chance to develop outstanding teamwork.

2. Discernment

Discernment is sensing the external and internal influences taking place in others and being sensitive to those influences. Discernment facilitates understanding the following questions:

1. What motivates the other person?
2. What are the other person's needs or desires?
3. What dynamics are occurring in the other person?
4. How can I create an empowered atmosphere to enable this relationship to grow?

3. Trust

Trust is absolute belief in the responsiveness of another. Honoring the trust of another human being is the foundation of relationships. Trust grows through listening, sharing, and confidentiality. Trust is the single most important factor in relationships.

4. Risk

Risk is making one's self vulnerable to disengagement from others by sharing personal information. When the conversation seems to have revealed common interests and seems comfortable, one may shift the conversation to a deeper, more personal level. People usually respond to another's level of candidness. There are three stages of risk: thinking (low), sensing (moderate), and active (high). Higher risks facilitate deeper levels of personal communication. For relationships to grow, individuals must move from the lower to the higher stages.

5. Truthfulness

Truthfulness is presenting one's story in accordance with reality. People who discern truthfulness in each other are inclined to listen and share what is really on their minds. They also feel they have each other's best interests at heart.

6. Teamwork

Teamwork is working interdependently with one another to reach a common goal. Interdependence is the state of standing on one's own efforts while working in harmonious relationships with others. Mutual interest plus commitment equals teamwork. Commitment is pledging in good faith one's determination to work with another.

This cycle continuously perpetuates itself in any given successful relationship. Teamwork is the goal of relationships. Once teamwork is achieved people can proceed with their missions. So let's analyze what teamwork can do.

Teamwork enhances spheres of influence as people identify the following:

1. Who I am
2. Who you are
3. Who we are together
4. What we do
5. How we do it

Teamwork facilitates leadership improvement cycles. The model that I recommend to illustrate this dynamic is the Linzey PIE Cycle in Figure 11 below.

Moral Leadership

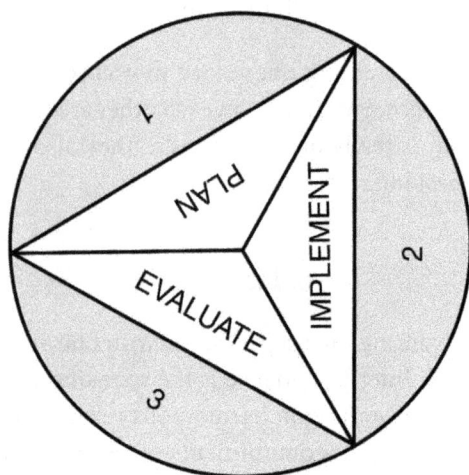

Figure 11. PIE Cycle

The Linzey PIE Cycle (Plan, Implement, Evaluate) is simpler than the Demming Wheel. It is circular in motion since it is repetitive in nature. Leadership improvement cycles are the basis of all systems of operations. The key elements to improve any system are as follows:

1. *Plan*: Plan the work. Determine why and how the work should be done.
2. *Implement*: Work the plan. Implement procedures to accomplish the objective.
3. *Evaluate*: Evaluate the results of the entire project from beginning to end.

Then analyze the collected information. Next, evaluate whether or not goals were reached, and determine why or why not. Then repeat the process with the new data in mind to build on established successes.

People subconsciously implement their own improvement system daily regarding any task they undertake. But it helps to conduct this process formally as a team on mission-essential tasks.

Team Leadership

This process enables people to intentionally improve any task, resulting in greater customer satisfaction and improved teamwork.

The Green Berets illustrate this principle. The Special Operations Command develops leaders by teaching them to assess situations realistically and then to develop action plans that address all the issues and draw on all available resources. For example,

> In the Spring of 1991, the Kurdish people of Northern Iraq rose up against Saddam Hussein. When the Iraqi army crushed their rebellion . . . hundreds of thousands of Kurds headed for the mountains that border Iraq and Turkey, and a massive tragedy awaited as the refugees began freezing and starving to death. The United States responded with Special Forces teams. Seventy men were dropped near one camp at night. The first morning they witnessed the food distribution disintegrate into a riot that ended with seven Kurds being shot by frightened Turkish forces. One Special Forces team of twelve men was sent into the camp of 150,000 to assess the situation. Although team members felt threatened, they knew that force was not a real option for accomplishing their mission. They brought back their diagnosis of the situation: The Turkish and Kurdish leaders were not cooperating, and the humanitarian non-governmental organizations (NGOs), such as the Red Cross and Doctors Without Borders, were being kept on the fringes. Special Forces teams met with each group. Then they brought the groups together. They devised a food distribution system, which the Kurds themselves implemented and felt responsible for and which used the services of the Special Forces and the NGOs. The Turks were kept informed and provided security.
>
> This group of seventy Special Forces soldiers—dropped in with virtually no briefing on how to deal with the situation—organized the camp and involved every group that was there. Within one week, the camp was meeting the basic human needs of 150,000 Kurds, and fatalities plummeted. Within three months, the Kurds resettled into their homes in Iraq."[5]

5. Cohen and Tichy, *Leading Beyond the Walls*, 144.

Moral Leadership

AUTHORITY AND CONFLICT RESOLUTION

Leaders are called to serve, but their mandate to influence and direct subordinates and their authority to resolve conflict remains and must be respected.

Conflict in relationships is normal. Conflict is a fact of life. Most conflicts are with those whom we love most deeply. Facing conflict transparently strengthens relationships. Barrett Smith, Associate Director of the Turner Clergy Center of the Pastoral Institute, and contributing author to *Beside Still Waters*, says, "If the parties remain engaged through the conflict, the heat generated brings something altogether new into being—a deeper trust and greater intimacy. Marriage, for example, at its best, is an equal yoking of partners where the relationship is strengthened by the hard work of communication and caring to the end that both partners are fulfilled."[6]

Effective leaders address conflict in the work force. Smith cites a pastor, Jackson Carroll, who mentions a growing concern in organizational conflict surrounding leadership and authority. He says that social and cultural trends have adversely affected the average person's concept of leadership and authority. These trends include:

1. Questioning fundamental beliefs about God.
2. Marginalizing the religious institution.
3. Increasing clergy's dependency on volunteers to do the work of the religious institution.
4. Emphasizing shared ministry between the clergy and the laity.

People today are increasingly behaving as though *they* grant authority to religious institutions and traditions, Holy Scriptures, and the clergy.[7]

---

6. Muse, *Beside Still Waters*, 76–77.
7. Ibid., 80–81.

People may not actually say that they believe they grant authority to their religious leaders. But if they behave as though they do, then conflict arises. One way people grant authority to religious leaders is when denominational polity determines that parishioners must vote on religious leaders' employment status in the parish. Many parishes have split over voting, because voting is a win/lose decision-making technique. Religious leaders in those parishes run by the congregational form of church government usually have little control over the organization's resources and are at the mercy of their parishioners for paychecks. The problem is that many people are not able to handle institutional finances, nor are they able to handle power over senior leaders. If their abilities have not been correctly ascertained, they should not be empowered in these ways. Judas Iscariot was such an individual; he obtained more power than he could responsibly handle. But Jesus knew Judas' abilities when he empowered Judas. The difference is that Jesus had a reason for empowering Judas. Church government should not empower such individuals unless it desires to "crucify" its own leaders.

Congregational governments can reduce religious leaders to the status of beggars. Leaders cannot lead with authority in such circumstances. Authority seems to be much more respected in parishes run by an Episcopalian type government, which determines that the parish's headquarters assigns clergy to local parishes. In these cases, clergy would not rely on parishioners' approval for paychecks. Consequently, they would be free to lead with greater authority and security and with fewer organizational conflicts. They could then lead more effectively.

Authority in both religious and secular arenas is challenged from time to time. Organizational conflict can occur anywhere. Jackson Carroll's studies have shown that even secular authority is questioned at times. People have taken their perspectives toward religious authority and carried them into the secular arena. Issues of contention in religious institutions often revolve around financial control. But in the corporate world, it is not debatable that senior leadership, not subordinates, controls resources. It is my opinion, therefore, that religious institutions are not as able as corporations to address and resolve conflict. Corporate leaders would have no authority to lead if their subordinates controlled their employment status and the finances of the company or institution. Such dynamics would lead to dysfunctional leadership and bad business. Subordinates would have the leverage in mercilessly challenging the leadership. In non-religious organizations, since the people are on the receiving end rather than on the giving end of the finances, the leadership is perceived to have authority over the people.

Fortunately, not everyone in religious institutions challenges authority. Otherwise, religious institutions would not be thriving as they are today. However, religious institutions would function more efficiently if their members had a clearer understanding of leadership and authority. Perhaps religious institutions and corporations could learn more about leadership and authority by benchmarking and analyzing leadership processes in each other's organizations. *Benchmarking* means "comparing and implementing management concepts from corporate neighbors." The willingness to exchange concepts with fellow professionals in any technical field would foster networking, pending no hidden agendas exist to solicit each other's business or attendance as next week's newest synagogue visitor. But, then, one might be surprised.

Also, in *Beside Still Waters*,[8] Smith shares one parishioner's observations about the health of the religious institution after reading Robert Kemper's *What Every Church Member Should Know about Clergy*. These lessons provide probable answers to conflict resolution between religious leaders and their parishioners. But I am broadening this scope of understanding by applying Kemper's observations to all corporations, including secular businesses, to help all leaders resolve conflict. These broadened lessons are as follows:

1. Organizations will resolve conflict and be healthier if they do things that increase trust between leaders and the people they lead.

8. Ibid., 82–83.

Team Leadership

2. Understanding is the key ingredient in developing trust. The key idea here is that people will trust what they understand, but not what they do not understand.
3. Two issues in the process of understanding are these: Who are we? and What are we trying to accomplish?
4. The people must be able to communicate openly and respectfully with each other.
5. The people must be able to accept differences and disagreements.
6. Conflicts must be resolved constructively so that losers are not castigated.

These observations are ideal. But they may not reflect everyone's reality. The key to turning the ideal into the real is to come back to the concept of envisioning the empowered environment. Again, this environment is where people fulfill their roles and know their boundaries, and where leaders select steps toward making their own vision, and their follower's visions, real.

Note below the Levels of Organizational Conflict (Figure 12). Edwin Chase originally designed it as "Levels of Church Conflict."[9] Chase is another contributing author to *Beside Still Waters* and founder of the Clergy Resource Center at the Pastoral Institute. I have modified Chase's table to benefit all leaders and all types of organizations.

Conflict Level	Mild	Moderate	High	Hostile
Nature of Conflict	Differences	Personalities	Win/Lose	Destruction of Other
Communication Type	Open Person to Person	Guarded Third Person	Closed Rumor/Innuendo	Distorted, Gossip, Letter Campaign
Solution Type	Consensus	Compromise	One Sided	Scapegoating
Anxiety Level	Low	Moderate	High	Unbearable
Emotion Level	Calm	Moderate	Reactionary	Hostile Outbursts
Resolvability	Resolvability	Fair	Poor	Rare
Intervention	No Intervention	Minimal Peer Intervention	Inside Leadership Intervention	Outside Intervention

Figure 12. Levels of Organizational Conflict

9. Ibid., 138.

Moral Leadership

To resolve conflict, leaders must ask themselves these questions:

1. Which individuals or subgroups are most strongly committed to the company's key values?
2. How intense and how broad is the conflict between these and other groups?

A leader's overriding concern must be that the resolutions of conflict reinforce the company's critical values. A leader must also identify conflicts that involve vital values and norms. To do this, a leader must have a strong commitment to those values. Because of this commitment, a leader cannot compromise the company's basic values—regardless of the conflict that may ensue. Negotiation may result in compromise and inconsistency. If so, the company's values may be marred seriously. Badaracco is right when he states that the leader's first commitment is to the organization as a whole.[10]

Effective leadership, rather than depending on charisma or inborn leadership qualities, is hard work.[11] As examples of the hard work of leadership, Drucker points out General MacArthur, Field Marshal Montgomery, or Alfred Sloan, the man who built and led General Motors from 1920 to 1955.[12] The leader sets the goals, sets the priorities, and sets and maintains the standards. He also must make some compromises. But before accepting a compromise, the true moral leader has thought through what is right and desirable for the company at this time. When a leader is able to see leadership as a responsibility rather than a privilege, then the proper relationship between authority and conflict resolution can take place.

---

10. Badaracco, *Presidential Character*, 86
11. Drucker, *Managing the Future*, 121.
12. Ibid.

seven

Communication Under Moral Leadership

COMMUNICATION IS THE ART of transmitting and receiving messages. To say that communication is comprised of both speaking and listening is not completely accurate, because communication is 70 percent non-verbal and 30 percent verbal. What one does not literally speak may be conveyed or emoted. What one does not hear may be felt or perceived, either visually or intuitively.

Non-verbal communication often stems from the presence leaders create, often resulting from the way they carry themselves. Mannerisms include choice of words, tone of voice, personality, and character. Dr. Stephen Muse, the Senior Pastoral Psychotherapist and Director of Counselor Training at the Pastoral Institute, illustrated this observation when he came to Fort Lee, Virginia, to speak to a group of military chaplains, civilian clergy and social workers. One of the topics he addressed was communication. He described one of his friends who had a flair for the dramatic and was at ease entertaining crowds. His friend said, "When my wife and I were in Las Vegas and Robert Goulet came on stage, his charisma filled up the whole place. My wife and I both recognized why he was a star."

Muse contrasted the personal charisma of Robert Goulet with that of Mother Theresa. Malcolm Muggeridge interviewed Mother Theresa on television in the 1960s. Muggeridge noted that Mother Theresa had no personal charisma about her. But after Muggeridge interviewed Mother Theresa, the phone lines were flooded with callers saying, "That woman spoke to my heart in a way no other person ever has!" Muse noted that Mother Theresa was able to communicate through deep, inner character that he described as "humility, goodness, and charity," which he says drew those who were listening to "the Shepherd's voice." Muse raised a good point by asking, "Ministers who lead with their personalities may be creating in the sheep a flair for the dramatic, but are they reaching the heart as did Mother Theresa?" Too often leading from the personality will eventually reach the skin of mankind; however, leading from the well of character will eventually reach the soul of humankind.

Natural-born leaders communicate with ease. Others, though, need to practice their communication skills. Consequently, this chapter shows how to communicate effectively. The information brief is the model. The techniques in preparing and delivering the information brief apply to most forms of public speaking. Speakers may want to modify the introduction of the information brief to suit their purposes. The chapter then concludes with tips on interpersonal communication.

PUBLIC SPEAKING

Public speaking is a powerful tool. When speaking, one presents ideas to numerous people. Since public speaking is a monologue and the speaker is not able to read listeners' minds, leaders must prepare their speeches to be certain that they will communicate well. Walter Ong, an expert on public speaking, says that speech is a window to the mind. For this reason, Dr. Erin DeMeester Reynolds, former Associate Professor of Communication, has taught her students at Fuller Theological Seminary to make sure the "window" they provide their audience when they speak is a view

Communication Under Moral Leadership

they want that audience to have. Military leaders provide powerful windows of themselves to their audiences by using active verbs rather than passive verbs. Active verbs accentuate the message. Speakers should avoid the "to be" verbs such as *is, was, be, being* and *been.* They should also avoid using main verbs ending with *-en.* For example, *ate* instead of *eaten* and *will write,* rather than *will be written* are preferred. Such choices will usually eliminate much of the passive mode and project the speaking into the active mode.

Four sources of feedback can reveal weaknesses and strengths in presentation and thus enhance a speaker's delivery:

1. Mirrors
2. Videotapes
3. Live feedback
4. Recorders.

The most outstanding feedback is the use of mirrors so that speakers can observe their mannerisms and instantly correct problems. Videotaping rehearsals and final presentations is an excellent source of feedback to ascertain what speakers actually do in front of audiences and how audiences respond. People's feedback after presentations is an excellent indicator of how speakers affected them. And recorders are excellent playback tools to develop natural expressions and inflections of the voice. Because most of us do not see or hear ourselves as others see or hear us, our perspective of our delivery is changed when we see our mannerisms and hear our inflections as others do.

Public speeches should normally range from twelve to twenty minutes. Speakers should always work within the attention span of the audience. It is always a good idea for speakers to find out how much time is allotted. Preachers should usually plan on twenty-minute sermons or less in churches. However, some news briefs in war zones might require only five minutes. Also, the U. S. President's State of the Union Address should probably last nearly an hour due to the comprehensive nature of the speech. The purpose of the speech determines the length.

All speakers should tell stories to illustrate their point. The art of storytelling is obvious when we consider the great speakers we have heard—almost all use stories to illustrate the main points. Also, we listen to and we remember the stories speakers tell. No one captivates an audience like an excellent storyteller. The most renowned speakers are known for telling great stories, because stories are interesting and great stories drive home the points the speakers want to make.

The essential steps to writing speeches and public presentations are these:

1. Define the purpose.
2. Analyze the audience.
3. Research the topic.
4. Support the material.
5. Organize the material.

Purpose. The military teaches three purposes for communication—direct, inform, or persuade. To direct emphasizes *what* to do, to inform emphasizes *how* to do it or *what* to know, and to persuade emphasizes *why* one should do it. In order to effectively fulfill the purpose for a presentation, a speaker must first determine that purpose.

Audience. Speakers should analyze the audience's culture, educational level, knowledge of the topic, and religious or ideological positions, as well as the personalities present. Speakers must adjust accordingly to reach the variety and diversity of the audience.

Research. Thorough research enables speakers to support the subject matter. It is a good idea to research and present the pros and cons of the topic. Doing so helps educate audiences about various perspectives. Audiences expect speakers to share personal perspectives as a means of encouraging them to draw their own conclusions. Audiences appreciate the respect. Sharing various perspectives before acknowledging one's own persuasion will *influence* the audience to take the speakers' perspectives more seriously.

Support. Support material includes statistics, references, illustrations, anecdotes, humor, news releases, personal experiences, and brief stories. Such support provides audiences with a psychological air of authenticity and helps them remember messages. Speakers should also support ideas by explaining *why*. People want to know *why*. Explaining *why* perfects the art of persuasion. Persuasion is the main objective in public speaking. But to inform is the objective in most military, collegiate, and industrial settings.

Organize. Speakers should first organize research material into the following typical main categories: topic, introduction of main points, main points, and sub points. Then they should add the conclusion, lessons learned, and closing statement. The conclusion is a restatement of the introduction with a brief summary of main points. Lessons learned are usually the two main insights gained during the research. The closing statement may be a short challenge or a brief quote relevant to the topic.

THE INFORMATION BRIEF

The United States military is a pioneer in developing the information brief. It is the most effective method of disseminating information to commanders and their staffs. Every young officer and non-commissioned officer must learn how to give information briefs as a basic tool to use throughout their careers.

The information brief is a speech designed to disseminate information to a military leader or CEO. Below is the format the military provides to facilitate this task with brevity. It is important for effective leadership since it requires the clearest flow of thought and its brevity saves time. Saving time saves money so that personnel can get back to the mission. Brevity also shows respect for the listeners and enhances the performance of speaking. Briefs vary in length depending on the topic. The structure of the information brief provides parameters, and effective leaders stay within them. Staying within the parameters compels one to edit down to the point of having the least material necessary to get the job done. The result is a lean and powerful presentation. The brief may be presented on paper, overhead transparencies, or PowerPoint presentations. PowerPoint is preferred.

Generally, information briefs should be no longer than thirteen to fifteen minutes. Time may vary depending on senior guidance. It is important that those delivering briefs should rehearse and time themselves. Unfamiliar subject matter may be typed in the notes section of the PowerPoint slide to stay on point. Placing materials in plastic covers or in binders keeps the material in order and makes pages easy to turn.

Information Brief Format

- *Introduction/Title (slide 1)*. Present name, title of presentation, and list date on the slide.
- *Purpose (slide 2)*. State the purpose, classification and type of brief in the infinitive. Here is an example, "To provide a bird's-eye perspective of the organizational structure of Company XYZ."
- *References (slide 3)*. List the material used in conducting the research. The Air Force lists the references on the title slide.
- *Outline (slide 4)*. The outline should list brief bullet topics to be covered.
- *Body (slides 5–24 approximately)*. Throughout the body of the brief, slides should be used for each main point and sub point. For numerous sub points, the one giving the brief should have an overview slide of the various sub points to be discussed under the main points. Necessary charts, diagrams, and illustrations will require extra slides. Transitional statements between main points are necessary for an effective flow of thought.

- *Conclusion (slide 25).* Restate and briefly summarize the main points from the main outline. No new material should be presented from this moment onward.
- *Lessons Learned (slide 26).* It is acceptable to insert a slide briefly stating two lessons learned from the research. The one presenting the brief should use no more than one or two sentences per lesson learned.
- *Questions (slide 27).* Show the question slide and ask for questions. In the Air Force format, "Are there any questions?" is actually asked after the closing statement with no slide.
- *Closure (slide 28).* Bring closure with a brief quote and its source.

INTERPERSONAL COMMUNICATION

Interpersonal communication differs in dynamics from public speaking. Personal relationships do not develop when one person is speaking to an audience but when people are speaking one on one. So when communicating with individuals, it is good to remember the rules of engagement below. Successful leaders follow these rules and relate well with anyone, about anything, anywhere.

1. Speakers should speak for themselves, rather than for others. Speaking for others might be perceived as presumptuous. If you are authorized to speak for another person, it would be to your benefit to preface your remarks by saying so.
2. Speakers should not dominate discussions. There is a difference between dominating discussions and being an extrovert who likes to talk. Domineering individuals sometimes project themselves due to an inferiority complex, so they strive to be the center of attention. Not only is this behavior unbecoming to leaders, but also it exposes their inferiority complexes. Such leaders should seek professional help or suffer quietly

inside rather than reveal their complexes at the expense of others and themselves.

3. Speakers should allow the listener to paraphrase often. Asking the listener to paraphrase what you are saying ensures that communication is really occurring. Simply going through the motions of communication without someone receiving or understanding the communication wastes time. Time is money. Paraphrasing allows the listener to request clarification on issues. Listeners should paraphrase the speaker to show they understand the point made. If speakers welcome you to paraphrase, accept the invitation. But if they inundate you with confusing information and do not give you an opportunity to request clarification, ask if you may paraphrase what you are hearing and then ask for clarification.

4. Listeners should not rebut. Listeners should seek first to understand. When it is their turn to speak, then they should communicate what they are hearing to convey any inaccuracies in understanding. When some listeners hear inaccurately, they may try to rebut points not intended to be part of the presentation. Finally, and only after they understand clearly, they should seek to be understood.

5. Speakers and listeners should share the floor. Sharing the floor may mean discussing one issue thoroughly before transitioning to the next item. It also means not dominating and not unloading a barrage of issues causing the listener to be overwhelmed.

The basic foundation of communication is trust. When trust collapses, communication turns to threats, blaming, or accusations; thus, decision making becomes defensive or protective rather than innovative and creative.[1] There can be no forward progress when trust is missing. Trust is the unification that holds teams together and helps colleagues work together in crises. Lynch has discovered, through his research, that there is "very strong

---

1. Lynch, *Leading Beyond the Walls*, 172.

evidence that high trust is the catalyst of very high performance, greater innovation, creativity, synergy, expansion of possibilities, enhanced problem resolution, faster action and implementation, lower litigation costs, and lower transaction costs."[2] Therefore, because trust improves performance to such a degree, companies and businesses (including the military and churches) cannot afford to ignore the necessity of developing trust in their leadership roles.

There is strong evidence that interpersonal communication skills can be improved dramatically through training. Every leader ought to know how to paraphrase, summarize, express feelings, disclose personal information, admit mistakes, respond nondefensively, ask for clarification, solicit different views, and so on. Such communication is not automatic or a result of inborn charisma. In fact, "Howard S. Friedman, professor of psychology at the University of California, Riverside, and his colleagues studied the communication of emotions from the perspective of nonverbal expressiveness. They found that those who were perceived to be charismatic were simply more animated than others. They smiled more, spoke faster, pronounced words more clearly, and moved their heads and bodies more often. They were also more likely to touch others during greetings. What we call *charisma*, then, can better be understood as human expressiveness."[3]

Flexibility is an important part of interpersonal competence. Leaders must be versatile enough to adopt a style that is appropriate to different situations and different people. Versatility expands one's capacity to function in a wide range of cultures and environments. The higher one advances in an organization, the more presentations one is likely to be required to give. Presentation skills are essential, especially the ability to appear at ease in front of an audience. According to Bert Decker, founder and president of Decker Communications, a nationwide communications training and consulting firm, people are more afraid of having to give

---

2. Ibid., 173.
3. Friedman, et al., *The Affective Communication Test*, 333–50.

a speech than they are of dying.[4] A course in public speaking will provide a person with self-confidence as well as with techniques for presenting material effectively.

Leaders must interact with their followers. General opportunities for interaction are important, but it is also important to meet one on one and face to face. Such face-to-face communication lets people know that leaders care about them personally. It will also improve the possibility of understanding with team members even when opposition is expected. Consulting one on one decreases the chance that leaders will be surprised by another's arguments or concerns at crucial times of growth or stress in the organization.[5] Some kind of action every day will ensure that leaders will interact with people they know and want to know better as well as with people they do not know and need to know.[6]

---

4. Decker, *You've Got to be Believed*, 155.
5. Kouzes and Posner, *Leadership*, 171–72.
6. Ibid., 172.

eight

Character Formation as Key to Moral Leadership

LEADERS ARE NOT BORN with more creative genius than other people, neither are they more intelligent nor filled with more ability. They are not preordained to be leaders. They are as human as everyone else. They make mistakes too. But they also learn from their mistakes. Leadership can be learned; in fact, it must be learned. We start learning the skills and techniques of leadership just as we learn self-understanding and the other knowledge skills of our professions.

A proverb tells us that "knowledge is power." It is true that some knowledge is essential for accomplishing any task. However, unless we add wisdom to our knowledge, the knowledge is impotent and we will accomplish little. Wisdom, according to Rick Joyner, is "the *ability* to apply knowledge correctly. Courage is the *will* to apply it."[1]

History shows us, as Joyner points out, that even the most outstanding leaders will ultimately fail unless their lives have the underpinnings of honor, morality, and character.[2] This assertion remains true even for the most brilliant of leaders. Some of the

---

1. Joyner, *Leadership, Management*, 55.
2. Ibid.

characteristics comprising this character in leaders are the will to implement the plan, to keep priorities, and to be steadfast, as well as to have endurance, integrity, courage, loyalty, and initiative.

Perhaps the first thing to look for in any kind of leader or potential leader is strength of character. Serious character flaws will eventually make a leader ineffective. Character flaws are not the same as weaknesses; they cannot be changed overnight. If change comes, it will take a long time. Some of the qualities that make up good character include honesty, integrity, self-discipline, teachability, dependability, perseverance, conscientiousness, and a strong work ethic. We can tell much about leaders by their ability to take responsibility for their actions, to honor their promises and obligations, and to meet their deadlines.

Steadfastness was originally a navy term for the ability to stay on course. It is also the ability to keep returning to the course when one gets off of it—whether on purpose or by accident. Endurance is the ability to stay with the task all the way to its completion. The ability to finish the job takes discipline. The failure to complete jobs is usually a sign that one is running on emotion rather than a vision.[3]

"A basic part of character is integrity. Trust is the foundation of all cooperative enterprise, and integrity is the basis of all trust," states Robert Porter Lynch.[4] Lynch is president of the Warren Company, which helps companies build alliances in a wide variety of industries. Integrity is more than being honest. It includes the actions of doing right. It is also being free of corrupting influences. We could say it is doing what our consciences tell us to do or standing up for our convictions.[5] In addition, integrity is what allows leaders to admit their mistakes and accept appropriate blame for them.

General Lee, for example, never blamed anyone else for his defeat at Gettysburg. His subordinates failed him several times during that battle, and the effect of those failures led Lee to make

---

3. Ibid., 59, 61.
4. Lynch, *Leading Beyond the Walls*, 171.
5. Joyner, *Leadership, Management*, 62.

decisions that led to the defeat. But Lee never mentioned his subordinates' failures. After the war, one general publicly blamed Lee for the defeat, and Lee agreed with him. This humility endeared him to the entire world, and he became a most respected man after the war—even among the Northerners. His humility and character proved him to be one of the great men of that era.[6]

Integrity is the ability to honor one's word, especially when it is hard to do so, and even when personal cost is involved. For Gerry Dehkes, of Lucent Technologies, "Integrity includes setting expectations and consistently meeting them. Doing both is important. . . . View problems as . . . opportunities to show your trustworthiness, meeting the expectations you've set with your partners."[7] Character formation is essential to effective leadership. From a secular standpoint, it prepares leaders for advancement and makes them better able to handle responsibility and understand themselves and human nature in general. From a moral or religious standpoint, it becomes a duty for all people to grow moral consciousness and become more cognizant of the Divine within their lives.

Character is moral fiber. Character formation is the process of changing one's disposition through inner disciplines. The following sections discuss these disciplines: Confession, Confidants and Small Groups, Beliefs, Unconditional Acceptance and Leadership Beatitudes.

CONFESSION

Confession is a deeply therapeutic ongoing process comprised of opening the soul to a trusted caregiver, experiencing intimate sharing of wrongdoing, and receiving forgiveness from one's God and self. Regardless of faith, values, and degree of faults, the ability to divulge shortcomings and moral failures to another human being in an atmosphere of complete acceptance promotes healing

---

6. Ibid., 62.
7. Lynch, *Leading Beyond the Walls*, 172.

of the soul. However, determining who would be a trusted confidant is a delicate process. Also, building a relationship of trust with another person to this degree of confidence may take considerable time. Some individuals are not capable of being trusted and would not know how to handle confession. Greater harm and the inability to ever trust are known to result from confessing to the wrong people.

CONFIDANTS AND SMALL GROUPS

Overall, clergy are the most sought after confidants. Those with a tradition of confidentiality and confession are the most sought after for the purpose of confession. Such traditions include the Orthodox Church, the Roman Catholic Church, the Anglican Church, the Lutheran Church, industrial chaplains, and the military chaplaincy. Military chaplains provide confidentiality in accordance with regulations, the Chaplains' Code of Ethics, and their faith traditions. Military personnel are entitled by law to privileged communication with chaplains. The privilege belongs to any military member who desires to speak with a chaplain. There is also a growing trend in corporations to hire chaplains for this purpose. People whose spiritual needs are met are more productive in fulfilling the mission of the corporation.

Mentors also serve as confidants. Everyone needs a mentor to whom accountability is required for personal and spiritual growth. This process strengthens individuals where they are weak and maintains their strengths.

Small groups may also provide an atmosphere of non-attribution where people feel safe enough to confess and grow. But this trust level depends on the nature and purpose of the small group. Everyone would benefit from being part of a growth group that fosters spiritual or personal growth and bonding with one another. Such groups are found in various places, such as clinics, campuses, and churches.

BELIEFS

Adherence to the traditional set of principles, beliefs, and faith demonstrates the desire to be faithful to one's God. Doing so helps build strong, exemplary leaders. To find acceptance from one's God is a spiritual reality that many long to have. This acceptance provides a strong moral base for character and leadership development. Such acceptance is also conveyed through humankind, showing God's acceptance through human acceptance. In order for individuals to truly grow and change, they must acquire self-acceptance before they can find acceptance in the eyes of others.

UNCONDITIONAL ACCEPTANCE

There is a trend among many in the helping professions to view people as in a process of "becoming," in terms of improving or striving to become something other than what they are. In other words, professionals often tell people that they are not acceptable according to the normative standard and must become better. This neurosis has infected Western culture. People must transcend this cultural disease in order to accept themselves and others unconditionally.

Likewise, many religious traditions have fixated their parishioners in the "becoming" frame of mind, rather than instilling within them the here-and-now unconditional self-acceptance.

People usually discover that mentally being in the here and now to their fullest psychological capacity is, in actuality, the secret to changing their realities. The result of true self-actualization is genuinely becoming who and what they wish to be. Unconditional acceptance of one's present condition is the key to change. There is no disputing the truth that people should change. The methodology of helping people to change is what is in question.

The most effective method of helping people to change is through unconditional acceptance. Regardless of who and what people are, they all must experience forgiveness for being human. All of us need to be forgiven as well as to forgive. And those who try to do the forgiving must have no hidden agendas to get others to become something that they are not.

Accepting people as they are does not imply that all their various value systems must be accepted. Some people believe that anything goes. While we can unconditionally accept people with unhealthy value systems as they are, we do not also have to accept their value systems. Love for our fellow human beings dictates that we point out the error of their ways so that they can know how and why to change. But acceptance requires that we allow them to learn healthy value systems at their own pace rather than pressure them to accept our value systems on our terms.

While stationed at Fort Lee, Virginia, I had the unique experience of offering unconditional acceptance to an Army soldier who was a minister in the Church of Satan. Our encounter enabled him to become more self-accepting and honest about his true beliefs. I have used a pseudonym to protect his true identity. Here is what transpired:

> On May 1, 2000, I was awakened at 2:15 a.m. with a phone call from the Emergency Operation Center. The staff duty officer informed me of a soldier's suicide attempt. Private Paul Nelson had just been transported to the Emergency Room at John Randolph Medical Center off post. He had overdosed on pills to make his heart stop beating. Fortunately, the soldier did not take enough pills to cause serious harm. The doctors pumped his stomach and said he was going to be all right. Then he was taken to the psyche ward for observation.
>
> Private Nelson and I had the opportunity to talk. He told me that he used to be a "Holy Roller," his mother being a minister in the Church of God in Christ. His peers picked on him mercilessly and treated him as an outcast throughout school. All the gangs treated him as an enemy, since he did not belong to any of them. Private Nelson refused to wear the gang's colors, rags, or hats in any of their respective ways. They could not identify with him, so they rejected, beat, and made fun of him for being a "Holy Roller." He forgave these kids over and over all his life until he became "sick of forgiving." Private

Nelson eventually found acceptance by some of his peers when he joined the Church of Satan—showing he was tough. Eventually, he became a minister in the Church of Satan. Then in 1998, he met a young Christian lady who became his high school sweetheart. At that time, she did not know he was in the Church of Satan. She became pregnant and they dreamed of getting married and settling in a cabin out of state. Eventually, she suffered a miscarriage. The tragedy was very grievous to them, but they managed to overcome their loss.

Private Nelson decided to join the Army to begin working toward supporting their dream of being together. Basic training at Fort Knox went exceptionally well for him. Then he was stationed at Fort Lee where he in-processed in the 244th Quartermaster Battalion, the largest battalion in the United States Army, to receive training in logistics and supply. Then the bottom suddenly fell out of everything he held dear to his heart. A third party from his home town informed him that his girlfriend had broken up with him because she discovered that he was a minister in the Church of Satan. He endured the emotional anguish for three weeks, until he felt he could not take it any longer. Then he decided to end his life.

As Private Nelson shared his life story with me, we connected. I knew about the gang environment, wearing of certain colors, and the whole scene he aptly described. I had taught school in the Watts district of Los Angeles for seven years and understood his background. I communicated unconditional acceptance. I conveyed that we all make wrong choices, but that God picks us up where we are and dusts us off to get us going again in the right direction. And probably the most significant statement I made was that I liked neither pious people nor pious religions that make a sham out of genuine worship. Instead, I emphasized relationship with God. Consequently, he was able to see that God had not given up on him and that God loved him unconditionally. I shook his hand and said, "You are set free. God wants to give you another start." Private Nelson's face lit up, his eyes widened, and he grinned from ear to ear. Without pressuring him, I asked him if I could pray for him before leaving, and he permitted me to do so.

A week later after counseling numerous soldiers in Private Nelson's barracks at Mike Company, I left for the evening to go home. It was sunset. As I walked down the sidewalk alongside the barracks, observing numerous soldiers playing basketball, I had walked past a certain soldier without realizing it. From behind me I heard a voice call out, "Chaplain." I turned around and saw Private Nelson sitting beside the barracks. He said, "Do you remember me?" I said, "Yes, Private Nelson." He simply said, "I believe." My eyes moistened. I'll never forget what he said.

He had been in the Church of Satan, not because he believed in it, but because he simply wanted acceptance. However, when I conveyed unconditional acceptance without trying to change him, he began accepting himself. Consequently the Church of Satan was no longer important to him.

Empowering people to experience unconditional acceptance is the key to their hearts, to breaking down barriers, and unleashing the forces of change to build and enhance character in their lives.

THE NINE LEADERSHIP BEATITUDES

These Nine Leadership Beatitudes ("be" attitudes) are attitudes leaders should display in their personality. Leaders should refer to them often, for these wise sayings will help them make it through the day.

1. Blessed are leaders who are continually considerate, understanding, and respectful to their team, for they will last long into the day.
2. Blessed are leaders who keep a sense of humor, for this quality will be a stress reliever to their team.

3. Blessed are leaders who see the good in others over and above the faults, for such leaders will expand their sphere of influence.
4. Blessed are leaders who are slow to judge, for they will reap a harvest of friends.
5. Blessed are leaders who make their environment a safe haven of trial and error, for their team members will become experts.
6. Blessed are leaders who spend ample time practicing their faith, for their faith will increase.
7. Blessed are leaders who seek first to understand and then to be understood, for they will communicate well.
8. Blessed are leaders who confront problems without becoming angry, for they will reap a harvest of peace.
9. Blessed are leaders who can forgive the hurts of the past, for their team will learn commitment.

Moral leaders treat everyone with respect, kindness, and honesty—in the same way they want to be treated. Through attitudes, judgments, humor, and communication skills, leaders are obliged to preserve the dignity of all workers and followers. Good leaders always pay attention to the human needs of their subordinates. That same consideration and honesty will also apply to all dealings with the public, with the government, with the media, with donors, workers, colleagues—anyone and everyone connected to the business.

Understanding leads to commitment. Leaders must assure their own and their groups' understanding of company principles, values, practices, and goals. Clear assumptions lead to clear understanding, which in turn leads to commitment. The more leaders are able to understand their followers, the more empathic those leaders become and the less likely they will have clashes in the group. Respect for others and honesty in dealing with others must remain constant. The consistency helps establish the sense of value that makes others worthy of respect.

Moral Leadership

Humor is as essential in work as it is in families and other relationships. When we cannot laugh at and with ourselves, we are preparing for a fall—physically, emotionally, or some other way.

Positive thinking, though not enough to run an organization or business by itself, often sets the standard by which successful companies operate. Never give up, but seek out opportunities and realize that most problems are not as bad as they seem—these are the key concepts to perseverance and to success. Maybe it would help us to remember the little train in the children's story—the one who continued to say, "I think I can, I think I can," and then finally could say, "I know I can."

Moral leaders will seek improvement in spiritual as well as human skills. Leaders need to be patient with themselves and with others. When leaders make judgments that are imperceptive or wrong, they must be able to admit the errors and allow followers a chance to be human as well as to allow themselves to be human. Forgiveness is necessary from both sides, as is leniency to risk at times, and leniency even to fail, especially in areas where trial and error may be an essential part of growth and success. Good leaders will make it possible for their followers to be prudent risk-takers. Responsible risks result in potential rewards. Leaders who recognize this are willing to experience failure so that they can experience success. Having confidence in themselves makes it easier for leaders to have confidence in their people—they will be quick to praise and encourage others in their organizations or on their teams.

Effective leaders believe in what they do because they have faith in themselves. Their faith gives them meaning and causes them to search, explore, and think creatively about the future, both for their personal lives and for their businesses. They have the internal strength necessary to guide their decisions. Their inner strength comes from the assurance that things could be better. And that assurance is part of the faith they have in their group and in themselves as leaders.

Trust is foundational to the survival of any organization. And, according to Jay Conger, the leader is responsible to create and maintain this trust.[8] The ability to deal with conflicts and disagreements depends on a healthy respect for differences. When leaders truly value people, the trust between those people and the leaders will develop and stay strong. Moral leaders trust others and are trusted by others. Trust holds any business or company together. In fact, an atmosphere of trust is so important that Badaracco and Ellsworth say it "enhances the flow of information through a company which ensures that top management is not sheltered from bad news and can respond to new and quickly changing environments."[9]

Trust and confidence are required for feedback, if such feedback is to result in the intended growth. Feedback is going to occur, so we need to know how to give it and how to receive it. Feedback is supposed to keep all of us on target, but feedback cannot be helpful or useful unless it is taken well and given with the proper motives. Trust is the key element—we must be able to trust the one giving the feedback so we know it is intended to help and not to hurt. In the same way, we must be trustworthy when we give feedback to others. We must give it honestly—to help someone rather than to satisfy some hidden motivation of our own. Trust influences productivity, relationships, and decision-making, for good decisions do not result from suspicion and distrust.

Leaders learn from correcting errors, as does everyone else. Our entire lives are learning experiences. Leaders are optimists and share a sense of hope with followers. Without that hope, there would be no reason to continue correcting errors and growing from mistakes.

When leaders confront the issues of disagreement and those who disagree with them, and when they expect their followers to do the same, they show respect for the abilities and judgments of other people. They show that they trust others to treat issues and people fairly. They also show the value of open communication. Effective leaders will know how to treat people, will recognize

---

8. Conger, *Spirit at Work*, 80.
9. Badaracco and Ellsworth, *Leadership and Quest for Integrity*, 121.

Moral Leadership

needs and will accept human nature as human. They will be able to get jobs done while helping people recognize their worth.

Constant communication with one's followers—influencing, encouraging, critiquing, and listening—will keep a leader in a position to understand, to be non-judgmental, to see the good in others rather than the negative, and to make followers feel secure in situations of trial and error and in circumstances requiring forgiveness.

Leadership is a daily pursuit for integrity. Leaders' behavior must be a consistent reflection of what they believe and what they expect of their organization. Integrity will help leaders develop their priorities and thus help guide them through difficulties and uncertainties. Poland's President Lech Walesa once told Congress that there was a declining market for words. The only thing the world believes, he said, "is behavior, because we all see it instantaneously."[10] Leadership involving values and attitudes attempts to overcome the superficial evaluation of people by actions and appearances only. Leaders with integrity need to look beyond the actions and behavior and act according to the values and attitudes that bring honor and trust to God and to co-workers.

Commitment to values also requires consistency. Values cannot rule through compromise. Inconsistent behavior sends mixed signals, thus increasing the insecurity of followers. Such behavior will also make the leaders appear to be manipulative and perhaps deceptive. Consistent behavior does not allow for misreading of the leaders' intentions. Values-driven leadership will motivate those working under that system of values. Values help workers feel that they are serving in worthwhile ways. The values of an organization must be clear; people cannot commit to vague or amorphous ideas that they cannot grasp.

Effective leaders know how to treat people, how to recognize and fulfill needs, and how to accept human nature as it is. They know how to get the job done while still helping people feel worthwhile.

---

10. Walesa, "The Year of the People," *Time*, 52.

IMPORTANCE OF CHARACTER

In speaking to people about leadership and looking through other books and articles on the subject, I couldn't help but notice that most of those people and books have a list of "requirements" or "essentials" for effective leadership. Interestingly enough, the items in these lists are different for each writer or speaker. Some factors overlap, of course, appearing on more than one person's list. However, in spite of these differences in the lists, one factor stands out because it appears in nearly all of them—the character/integrity issue. Without exception, every writer put integrity and character in the top lists of essentials for leadership. All concur regarding the importance of moral leadership.

It is easy to look around at our world today and jump to the conclusion that no one cares about character anymore. However, in the *Wall Street Journal*, October 31, 2003, there was an advertisement for a new book. The huge, bold headline stated "CHARACTER STILL COUNTS." The book being advertised was *Authentic Leadership: Rediscovering the Secrets to Creating Lasting Value*, by Bill George who is former Chairman and CEO of Medtronic. I have not read the book, but the concept of character is typical. This belief about the importance of character is becoming more and more significant for leaders.

James M. Kouzes and Barry Z. Posner, in their article "Seven Lessons for Leading the Voyage to the Future," also make the definite statement that "character counts." They point out that what most people are looking for in a leader is someone they would willingly follow. Those people looked for, in fact required, that anyone they would have confidence enough to follow must be "honest, forward-looking, inspiring, and competent."[11] Experts classify these kinds of traits as "source credibility" or, in laymen's terms, character traits. We want leaders we can believe in, whose word is trustworthy, who stand for something, and have the courage of their convictions. If leaders are not clear about what they believe, they will likely change their positions with new fads or

---

11. Kouzes and Posner, *Credibility*, 102.

new opinion polls.[12] Therefore, we demand that our leaders have the character that we can trust.

True, leaders are evaluated on what they accomplish and how they go about accomplishing it. But more than anything, these accomplishments will be outgrowths of the content of the leader's own character. Alfred C. Decrane, Jr., stipulates in "A Constitutional Model of Leadership" in The Drucker Foundation's *The Leader of the Future* that leaders must have "knowledge of their duty, and a sense of honor in action."[13] He further states, "real leaders are fair and honest . . . ; they are ethical, open, and trustworthy. These basic roots of character, perhaps more than any others, garner the respect that is needed in order for an individual to be called a leader."[14]

Decrane qualifies his strong statement by adding that short-term leadership can take place without these qualities, but any long-term or lasting leadership success "is impossible without them."[15] And long-time coach John Wooden is famous for his statement that ability may get you to the top, but it takes character to keep you there.

Part of the character of leaders shows up in the fact that they do not pursue their objectives at any and all costs without regard to *how* they achieve them. Integrity of character is first and most essential for moral leaders in business or any other field. "As a former head of the New York Stock Exchange once said, 'The public may be willing to forgive us for mistakes in judgment, but it will not forgive us for mistakes in motive.'"[16]

---

12. Ibid., 103.
13. Decrane, *Leader of the Future*, 249-56.
14. Ibid., 251.
15. Ibid.
16. Ibid., 252.

nine

Conclusion

WE ARE LEADERS. LEADERS are people who nurture life wherever they find it. Human life is the most valuable commodity we have. It is a sacred trust, and it is subject to our care. We have a tremendous responsibility to tend to the welfare of human life in all strata of society and in all spheres of influence.

Leadership *influences* human life through productive relationships and *directs* people through relevant communication, which *produces* teamwork. Teamwork produces decisions in the best interests of one's sphere of influence. Public speaking and interpersonal communication encompass skills that anyone can successfully employ with the right techniques and intent.

People who nurture their own lives through spiritual disciplines have the ability to encourage others to be people of character. Character empowers those who successfully emulate the Nine Traits of Moral Leaders, which have withstood the test of time.

In closing, I would like to say that one of the most important things we do in life, to be effective leaders among others, is to associate ourselves with people of good character if we value our own reputations. Otherwise, it is much better to be alone.

Appendix

Personal Mission Statement

THE FOLLOWING STEPS IN this Personal Mission Statement will enable you to be proactive in obtaining guidance for your life. An effective Personal Mission Statement is based on a Vision Statement. A Vision Statement includes three elements:

1. What kind of person you want to be, in terms of what character strengths you want to have, and what qualities you want to develop.
2. What you want to do, in terms of what you want to accomplish, and what roles you wish to fulfill in your life.
3. What you want to acquire in terms of ownership or power.

It is easy to list the character strengths you wish to develop. This list may be long. Power and fulfillment in life are based on who you are, what you are, and what you do, rather than what you acquire. However, since what you do often results in what you acquire, you need to include the things you wish to acquire in your Personal Vision Statement.

Appendix

STEP 1

Write a Personal Vision Statement based on who you want to be, what you want to become, what you want to do, and what you want to acquire.

STEP 2

Identify an influential person in your life. An effective way to focus on who you want to be, what you want to become, and what you want to do is to identify a highly influential individual in your life and describe how this individual has impacted your life. This person may be a leader, a work associate, a friend, relative, or neighbor. Please answer the following questions, keeping in mind your personal goals of who you want to be, what you want to become, and what you want to do.

1. Who has influenced my life more than anyone else?
2. What character traits do I admire in this person and desire to implement in my life?

STEP 3

Define your life roles. You may have roles in your life, family, work, and community. These roles are a natural framework to determine who you want to be, what you want to become, what you want to do, and what you want to acquire.

By identifying your life roles, you will gain perspective and balance. By writing these descriptive statements, you will begin to visualize your greatest potential. You will also identify the core principles and values by which you live. Examples of life roles are son, brother, husband, father, leader, teacher, manager, friend, administrator, employee, little league coach, volunteer, etc. List up to seven roles. Envisioning your future, describe how you will be involved in each role.

STEP 4

Write a rough draft of your Personal Mission Statement using the information you have provided in the first three steps. Next, edit it carefully to accurately reflect who you are, what you are, and what you do.

STEP 5

Write a final draft. After writing the final draft of your Personal Mission Statement, memorize both your Personal Vision and Mission Statements. Memorizing them will keep you moving toward your character-based goals.

STEP 6

Evaluate. A quarterly review and reevaluation of your Personal Mission Statement is required to ensure its accurate reflection of your life. A systematic review will also reflect your personal and professional development. When you review your Personal Mission Statement, ask yourself the following:

1. Is my Personal Mission Statement based on principles—unchanging rules of life? These principles are as follows:
2. Does my Personal Mission Statement accurately reflect who and what I really am at this stage in my development?
3. At my worst moments, does my Personal Mission Statement continue to reflect who and what I am?
4. Does my Personal Mission Statement provide me with a sense of direction?
5. Which leadership traits will enable me to accomplish my mission?
6. Do I need to make internal changes in my life to achieve my goals? If so, what are they?

Bibliography and Recommended Reading

Adler, Mortimer. *Six Great Ideas*. New York: Macmillan, 1981.
Air Force Quality Institute. *Quality Air Force Leaders Course*. Maxwell AFB, AL, 1996.
———. *Quality Team Member Training*. Maxwell AFB, AL, 1993.
Army Core Values. United States Army Basic Training Operating Instructions. http://usmilitary.about.com/library/milinfo/arbasicpol/blcorevalues.htm, 1.
Ashcroft, John. "Moral Leadership in Politics (or the Judiciary?)" *Mediafax Technologies, Inc.*, 1997, 1–4.
Badaracco, Joseph L. Jr., and Richard Ellsworth. *Leadership and the Quest for Integrity*. Boston: Harvard Business School Press, 1989.
Barber, James David. *The Presidential Character: Predicting Performance in the White House*. Englewood Cliffs, NJ: Prentice-Hall, 1977. Also see James D. Barber, "Adult Identity and Presidential Style: The Rhetorical Emphasis," *Philosophers and Kinds: Studies in Leadership*, ed. Dankwart A. Rustow. New York: George Braziller, (1970): 367–97.
Blitzer, R. J., C. Petersen, and L. Rogers. "How to Build Self-Esteem." *Training and Developmental Journal*, Feb. 1993, 59.
Burns, James MacGregor. *Leadership*. New York: HarperCollins, 1978.
Burwash, Peter. *The Key to Great Leadership: Rediscovering the Principles of Outstanding Service*. Badger, CA: Torchlight, 1995.
Cohen, Eli, and Noel Tichy. "Leadership Beyond the Walls Begins with Leadership Within." In *Leading Beyond the Walls*, eds. Frances Hesselbein, Marshall Goldsmith, and Iain Somerville. The Drucker Foundation Wisdom to Action Series. San Francisco: Jossey-Bass, (1999): 133–45.
Conger, Jay A. "Reuniting Spirituality and Work." *Spirit at Work: Discovering the Spirituality in Leadership*. Eds. Jay A Conger and Associates. The Jossey-Bass Management Series. San Francisco: Jossey-Bass, 1994.
Copenhaver, Marvin. *To Begin at the Beginning*, Cleveland: United Church Press 248 1994.

Bibliography and Recommended Reading

Covey, Steven. *The Seven Habits of Highly Successful People.* New York City: Simon & Schuster, 1989.

Crainer, Stuart. *The 75 Greatest Management Decisions Ever Made.* San Francisco: AMACOM American Management Association 90 1999.

Dale, Robert D. *Ministers as Leaders.* Nashville: Broadman Press, 1984.

Decker, B. *You've Got to Be Believed to Be Heard.* New York: St. Martin's Press, 1993.

Decrane, Alfred C., Jr. "A Constitutional Model of Leadership." *The Leader of the Future*, eds. Frances Hesselbein, Marshall Goldsmith, Richard Beckhard. Drucker Foundation Future Series. San Francisco: Jossey-Bass (1996): 249–56.

Drucker, Peter F. *Managing for the Future: The 1990s and Beyond.* New York: Truman Talley, 1993.

Eden, Dov. *Pygmalion in Management: Productivity as a Self-Fulfilling Prophecy.* New York: Lexington, 1990.

Eden, Dov. "Leadership and Expectations: Pygmalion Effects and other Self-Fulfilling Prophecies in Organizations." *The Leadership Quarterly* 3 (1992): 271–305.

Felder, Leonard. *The Ten Challenges.* Interview, April 1996. New York: Three Rivers (1997): 172–73.

Field, R. H. G. and Van Seters, D. A. "Management by Expectations (MBE): The Power of Positive Prophecy." *Journal of General Management* 14 2 (1988): 1–33.

Foucault, Michael. *History of Sexuality.* Eds., Robert Aldrich and Gary Witherspoon (2001): 93.

Friedman, H. S., L. M. Prince, R. E. Rigio, and M. R. DiMatteo. "Understanding and Assessing Nonverbal Expressiveness: The Affective Communication Test." *Journal of Personality and Social Psychology* 39 (1980): 333–51.

Gardner, J. W. *The Moral Aspect of Leadership*, Leadership Papers No. 5 (Washington D.C.: Independent Sectors, 1987), 10–18; see also R. W. Terry, *Authentic Leadership.* San Francisco: Jossey-Bass, 1993.

Garlikov, Rick. "Moral and Spiritual Values." http://www.garlikov.com/teaching/spiritual.html: 1–3.

George, Bill. "Authentic Leadership: Rediscovering the Secrets to Creating Lasting Value." *Wall Street Journal*, October 5, 2003.

Haas, Howard G. *The Leader Within: An Empowering Path of Self-Discovery.* New York: HarperBusiness, 1992.

Harmin, Merrill. "Value Clarity, High Morality: Let's Go for Both." *Educational Leadership* (1988): 24–30.

Heart, Bear and Molly Lankin. *The Wind is My Mother.* New York: Clarkson Potter (1996): 230–32.

Hill, Andrew, with John Wooden. *Be Quick—But Don't Hurry!: Finding Success in the Teachings of a Lifetime.* New York: Simon & Schuster, 2001.

Hof, Robert D. "How to Hit a Moving Target." *Business Week*, Aug. 21-28 (2006): 79.

Bibliography and Recommended Reading

Jones, E.C. "Interpreting Interpersonal Behavior: the Effects of Expectancies." *Science* 234 (1986): 41-46.

Joyner, Rick. *Leadership, Management, and the Five Essentials for Success.* Charlotte, NC: MorningStar 1994.

Korn/Ferry International and Columbia University Graduate School of Business. *Reinventing the CEO,* New York: Korn/Ferry International and Columbia University, 1989. Updated 2000: 90.

Kouzes, James M., and Barry Z. Posner. *Credibility: How Leaders Gain and Lose it, Why People Demand it.* San Francisco: Jossey Bass, 1993.

———. *The Leadership Challenge: How to Keep Getting Extraordinary Things Done in Organizations.* San Francisco: Jossey Bass, 1987.

———. "Seven Lessons for Leading the Voyage to the Future." In *The Leader of the Future: New Visions, Strategies, and Practices for the Next Era,* eds. Frances Hesselbein, Marshall Goldsmith, and Richard Beckhard. The Drucker Foundation Future Series. San Francisco: Jossey-Bass (1996): 99–110.

Lukes, Steven. *Power: A Radical View.* London: Macmillan Press (1974): 15–25.

Lynch, Robert Porter. "How to Foster Champions" in *Leading Beyond the Walls,* eds. Frances Hesselbein, Marshall Goldsmith, and Iain Somerville. The Drucker Foundation Wisdom to Action Series. San Francisco: Jossey-Bass, 1999, 167–88.

MacArthur, Douglas. *Washington Times.* May 27, 2002.

Mostert, Mary, ed. and analyst. "Voices From America's Past." *What True Americanism Demands of the American Citizen.* The Reagan Information Exchange, 2002.

Muse, J. Stephen. *Beside Still Waters.* Macon: Smyth and Helwys, 2000.

O'Toole, James. *Leadership A to Z: A Guide for the Appropriately Ambitious.* San Francisco: Jossey-Bass, 1999.

Peters, T. J. and N. Austin. *A Passion for Excellence: The Leadership Difference.* New York: Random House (1985): 290.

Peterson, C. and L.M. Bossio. *Health and Optimism: New Research on the Relationship Between Positive Thinking and Physical Well-Being.* New York: Free Press, 1991.

Pinchot, Gifford. "Creating Organizations with Many Leaders." *The Leader of the Future, New Visions, Strategies, and Practices for the Next Era.* Eds. Frances Hesselbein, Marshall Goldsmith, and Richard Beckhard. The Drucker Foundation Future Series. San Francisco: Jossey-Bass (1996): 25–39.

Pines, M. "Children's Winning Ways." *Psychology Today* 18 (1984): 58-65.

Rusoff, Jane Wollman. "Making the Team Work." *Research* (2006): 42-46.

Schwarzkopf, H. Norman. "Ethical Leadership in the 21st Century." Reprinted from *IMPRIMIS* n.d.

Senge, Peter. *The Fifth Dimension: The Art and Practice of the Learning Organization.* New York: Doubleday (1990): 206.

Bibliography and Recommended Reading

Smart, Bradford D. *Topgrading: How Leading Companies Win by Hiring, Coaching, and Keeping the Best People*. Paramus, New Jersey: Prentice Hall (1999): 377.

Tan, Paul Lee. *Encyclopedia of 7700 Illustrations: Signs of the Times*. Cleveland, TN: Assurance Publishers, 1990.

Thatcher, Margaret. "The Moral Foundations of Society." Speech reprinted by permission from *IMPRIMIS*, the monthly journal of Hillsdale College, 1994.

Thomas, Cal. "Speech at the Heritage Foundation." Washington D. C., October 31, 1996.

Tjosvold, C.W. and M. M. *Leading the Team Organization: How to Create an Enduring Competitive Advantage*. New York: Lexington Books (1991): 34.

Walesa, Lech. "The Year of the People." *Time*, Jan 1, 1990: 52.

Walton, Clarence C. *The Moral Manager*. Cambridge: Ballinger, 1988.

Subject Index

Ability, 3, 14, 28, 35, 38, 46, 48–49, 54, 56–57, 59, 75, 83, 85, 87, 133–135, 143, 146
Absolutes, 21, 22, 105
Acceptance, 8, 135–140
Actions, 1–2, 4, 8, 12, 15–16, 20–21, 23, 29, 32, 35, 37, 39, 44, 46, 48, 52, 55, 58–59, 68–69, 82–83, 85–86, 88, 90–91, 104, 134, 144
Adams, John, 5
Adaptability, 67, 94
Adler, Alfred, 58
Adler, Mortimer, 89
Adversity, 49, 52, 64, 91
Advice, 28, 35, 73, 80, 95, 100
Allen, Bob, 12
American civilization, xx
American colonists, 5
American culture, xi
American founding history, 4
American presidents, 4
Amoral, 2, 14, 22
Analyze, 58–59, 72, 76, 96, 115–116, 126
Apollo 13, 65
Aristotle, 5
Ashcroft, John, 7
Attitude, 15, 27, 30, 36, 42, 51, 54–56, 63–64, 66, 68–69, 75, 78–79, 83, 140, 144
Audience, 124–129, 131
Authority, 30, 57, 59, 61, 63, 68, 73, 80, 95, 106, 109, 111, 118–120, 122

Badaracco and Ellsworth, 85, 122, 143
Balance, 17, 23, 36, 55, 62–63, 101, 150
Barber, James David, 3–4
Bear Heart, 40
Bearing, 80
Behavior, 8, 34, 46
Beliefs, 40, 46, 49, 58–59, 84–85, 105, 118, 135, 137
Believability, 46
Bernstein, Ted, 35
Bezos, Jeff, 25
Bible, xi, 5, 12–14
Blanchard, Kenneth, 56
Bonding, 96, 136
Brainstorm, 31, 41, 47
Burns, James MacGregor, 2, 91
Burwash, Peter, 51

Caesar, Julius, 70
Capability, 33, 75, 78, 106
Carroll, Jackson, 118–119
Challenges, 8, 34, 36, 51, 77, 80, 92
Change, xviii–xix, 8, 18, 22, 26–27, 36, 38–40, 44, 49, 59, 65, 67, 72, 84, 92–95, 108, 134, 136–138, 140, 145, 151
Chaplain's Code of Ethics, 136

Subject Index

Character ethic, xviii, xix
Character, xii, xviii–xix, xx, 8–10,
  17, 21–24, 29–32, 35, 48, 51, 53,
  56, 64, 69, 75–76, 78–79, 89–92,
  94, 105, 123–124, 133–137, 140,
  145–147, 149, 150
Character formation, 79, 133–146
Characteristics, 2, 7, 31, 55, 91
Charisma, xviii–xix, 56–57, 65, 69,
  122–124, 131
Christianity, 14, 61
Churchill, Winston, 69
Clergy, 118–119, 123, 136
COA, 97, 101, 104
Coercion, 57, 61
Commanders, 69, 73, 127
Commitment, 19, 25, 27, 35–36,
  44, 46, 51, 81–83, 99, 115, 122,
  141, 144
Communicate, xx, 29, 39–40, 75,
  107, 121, 124, 130
Communication, 27, 36, 40, 42, 74–
  75, 79, 86–87, 96–97, 113–114,
  118, 123–124, 126, 129–132, 136,
  141, 143–144, 147
Community, 8, 14–15, 17, 29, 36,
  98, 150
Compassion 43, 85, 91
Competence, 19, 48, 63, 75, 131
Competitive, 25, 50, 86, 94
Compromise, 35, 98, 122, 144
Confession, 79, 135–136
Confidants, 135–136
Confidence, 8, 29, 33, 37, 47, 55, 79,
  92, 94, 106, 136, 142–143, 145
Conflict, 27, 34, 61, 80, 118–122,
  143
Conflict resolution, 96, 118, 120,
  122
Confucius, 52
Conger, Jay, 143
Consensus, 97–99
Considerate, 2, 42–43, 140
Consideration, 42–44, 48–49, 69,
  105, 141

Consistency, 34, 46, 70, 85, 88, 141,
  144
Constitution, U.S., 5, 7–8, 12
Constitutional model, 7–8, 92
Constitutional republic, 7
Consultation, 79
Consulting, 132
Control, 7, 12, 15, 29–31, 35, 52,
  56–57, 60, 62–63, 71, 106, 119
Coolidge, Calvin, 4–5, 9–10
Cooperation, 5, 27, 93–94
Core, 36, 58, 92
Core mission, 18, 100
Core principles, 7, 92, 150
Core qualities, xx, 8, 92
Core values, 89–91, 96
Corporate, 10, 32, 54, 81, 84, 106,
  118–120
Counseling, 76–77, 79
Country, 7, 10–13, 17, 20, 44, 81,
  86, 91–92
Courage, 5, 89, 91, 105, 133–134
Course of action, 73, 76, 97–98,
  101–103
Covey, Steven, 36
Crainer, Stuart, 36
Creativity, 30, 40–41, 87, 131
Credibility, 46, 145
Crisis, 44
Criticism, 55, 63, 81
Culture, 1, 9, 20, 126

Dale, Robert D., 17, 100
Decision-making, xviii–xix, xx, 41,
  60–61, 72, 76, 84, 96–97, 99, 105,
  119, 130, 143
Decision-making techniques,
  96–104
Decision Matrices, 101–104
  Figure 2, Raw Data Matrix, 101
  Figure 3, Relative Values Matrix
    (unweighted), 102
  Figure 4, Relative Values Matrix
    (weighted), 103
  Figure 5, Multiplication Matrix

Subject Index

(unweighted), 103
Figure 6, Multiplication Matrix (weighted), 104
Decisions, 35, 44, 55, 61–62, 75, 77, 82, 85, 96–99, 101–105, 107, 135, 142–143
Decisiveness, 82
Decker, Bert, 131
Declaration of Independence, 10–11, 81
Decrane, Alfred, 7, 92, 146
Define, 1–2, 18, 22, 29, 56, 59, 90, 100, 126, 150
Dehkes, Gerry, 135
Delegate, 57, 62, 76
Delegated authority, 57
Dependable, 17, 102
Dependability, 83, 134
Desires, 23–24, 35, 39, 114, 119
Directing, 72–73
Direction, 27, 38, 65, 73, 75, 78, 92, 151
Discernment, 114
Discipline, 14, 24, 29, 58, 134
Domination, 58, 60
Dowding, Kenneth, 58
Dreadnaught, 26
Dreams, 19, 38–39, 49, 51, 74
Drucker Foundation, 146
Drucker, Peter, 27, 69–70, 122
Drummond, Henry, 37
Duke University, 3
Duty, 46, 90–91, 105, 135, 146
Dynamic relationships, xx
Dynamics, 58, 114, 120, 129

Edison, Thomas, 51, 67
Effective, xii, xx, 3, 8, 19, 23, 28, 32, 35, 37, 39, 47–48, 52–53, 60, 62, 65, 68–70, 73–76, 80–81, 84, 87, 92–93, 96, 105, 108, 118, 122, 127–128, 135, 137, 142, 144–145, 147, 149–150
Effectiveness, 23, 63, 111
Ego, 35, 55, 62, 66

Egotism, 54–55, 95
Einstein, Albert, 41, 51
Empower, xvii–xviii, xx, 33, 56, 74, 97, 147
Empowerment, 36, 56, 106–107, 110–111, 121
Enable, 82, 96–97, 106, 108, 112, 114, 126, 138, 149, 151
Enabling, 18, 76, 108
Encourage, 27, 40, 65, 70, 95, 110, 142
Endurance, 31, 50–51, 83, 134
Energy, 65, 67, 84
Enthusiasm, 11, 66, 84, 87, 93
Environment, 7, 32, 58, 80, 92, 106, 108, 121, 131, 141, 143
Envision, 18, 38–39, 41, 48, 107
Ethical, xviii, xx, 12, 32, 34, 36–37, 49, 53, 75, 85, 88, 91, 104–105, 146
Ethical Decision-Making, 104
Ethics, xviii, 11, 19, 32, 35–37, 86, 88, 90, 105
Evaluate, 32, 35–36, 63, 82, 101–104, 106, 116, 146, 151
Executive leadership, 73, 78
Expertise, 50, 57, 63, 99, 106
External, 31, 53, 64, 72, 114

Facts, 37, 45–46, 62, 81
Fairness, 9, 85, 105
Faith, 5, 10, 45–49, 64, 90, 94, 115, 135–137, 141–142
Faithful, 45–46, 48
Faithfulness, 47–48
Family, 6–7, 46, 64, 70, 86, 112, 150
Fear, 1, 44, 54, 69, 91, 106
Feedback, 78–79, 96, 125, 143
Figures
Figure 1, Pyramid of Success, 93
Figure 2, Raw Data Matrix, 101
Figure 3, Relative Values Matrix (unweighted), 102
Figure 4, Relative Values Matrix (weighted), 103

159

Subject Index

Figure 5, Multiplication Matrix (unweighted), 103
Figure 6, Multiplication Matrix (weighted), 104
Figure 7, Traditional Leadership Paradigm, 110
Figure 8, Empowerment Leadership Paradigm, 110
Figure 9, Spherical Leadership Paradigm, 111
Figure 10, Relationship Dynamics Wheel, 113
Figure 11, PIE Cycle, 116
Figure 12, Levels of Organizational Conflict, 121
Flexibility, xix, 131
Force, 28, 40, 57, 61, 63, 72, 76
Ford, Henry, 42
Forgive 137, 141, 146
Forgiveness, 135, 137, 142, 144
Foucault, Michel, 59–60
Founding fathers, 5, 7, 9, 12–13
Four Stages of Empowerment, 107
Framers, 7–8, 92
Freedom, 4–6, 9, 24, 47
Friedman, Howard S., 131
Friendship, 34, 63, 93–94
Fundamental laws, 6

Game Theory, 58
Gandhi, Mahatma, 56
Gardner, John 28
Garlikov, Rick, 20
Gates, Bill, 42
General Motors, 70, 122
Gentleness, 52
George, Bill, 10, 146
Gettysburg Address, 11
Gibbon, Sir Edward, 5
Gideon, 95
Goal(s), 8, 19, 24–25, 28–29, 38, 44, 49–51, 64, 66, 70, 75, 78–79, 82–83, 87, 90–91, 97, 112, 115–116, 122, 141, 150, 151
God, 5, 12–14, 16, 19, 86, 118, 135, 137, 139, 144
Goodness, 69, 89, 124
Goulet, Robert, 123–124
Government, 2, 5, 7, 9, 12, 16, 44, 119, 141
Gramsci and Althusser, 60
Great Migration, 5
Green Bay Packers, 70
Green Berets, 117
Gretzky, Wayne, 42
Grow, 18, 28, 32, 63, 67, 69, 79, 94, 109, 114, 135–137
Growth, 9, 23, 28–31, 40, 44, 46, 50, 63, 67, 79–80, 94, 109, 132, 136, 142–143
Guide, 7, 78–79, 90, 92, 98, 142, 144
Guidelines, 22, 98

Hamilton, 7
Harmin, Merrill, 3
Harvard Business School, 25
Heroism, 69
Hof, Robert D., 25
Honest, 3, 32–36, 46, 88, 134, 138, 145–146
Honesty 23, 32–34, 48, 80, 85, 88, 94, 134, 141
Honor, 6, 13, 71, 90–91, 94, 105, 133–134, 144, 146
Hope, 19, 39, 87, 143
Human nature, 53, 135, 144
Humility 36, 52–52, 55–56, 62, 81, 124, 135
Humor, 100, 127, 140–142

Imagination, 40–42
Imaginative, 29, 32, 40–41
Implement, 78, 108, 116, 120, 131, 134, 150
Impression, 80
Improve, 18, 26, 28, 32, 63, 65, 108, 116–117, 132
Improving Your Serve, 108
Independent, 25, 31
Individualistic, 24–26, 28–29

Subject Index

Individuality, 24-25
Influence, xiii, xvii-xviii, xx, 31-33, 57, 61, 72-74, 77, 83, 106, 112-115, 118, 127, 141, 143, 147, 150
Information, 21, 55, 62-63, 78, 86, 102, 114, 116, 130-131, 143, 151
Information brief, 124, 127-128
Initiative, 29, 31, 75, 94, 134
Innovate, 18, 130
Innovation, 9, 25-29, 63, 131
Innovative, 26-29, 31-32
Integrity, xi, 4, 12, 22, 32-38, 45-46, 70, 81, 84-85, 90-91, 94, 105, 134-135, 144-146
Intemperate, 29
Interactions, 34, 59
Interactive, 54, 61, 63, 132
Interdependence, 115
Interests, 19, 27, 37, 61, 63, 72, 97, 105, 114-115, 147
Internal, 26, 60, 72-73, 114, 142, 151
Interpersonal, 28, 86
Interpersonal communication, 124, 129, 131, 147
Interpret, 8, 76, 92

Jacobi, Peter, 36
Jesus, 14-15, 119
Johnson, Lyndon, 4
Joyner, Rick, 6, 133
Judas Iscariot, 119
Judeo-Christian, 4, 13
Judgment, 20, 34, 54, 85-86, 141-143, 146
Justice, 5-6, 9, 89

Kemper, Roger, 120
Kennedy, John, 4, 24
Kindness, 43, 141
King, Martin Luther, Jr., 39
Knowledge, 3, 10, 26-28, 57, 59, 75, 77, 82, 85-86, 126, 133, 146
Kouzes, James and Posner, Barry, 2, 18, 34, 145

Leadership, 1-4, 7-12, 16-26, 28, 32, 35-36, 38-39, 43, 48, 50, 52-56, 58, 60, 65-66, 69-70, 72-73, 75-81, 83-87, 89, 91-92, 94-96, 106, 109, 111-112, 115-116, 118-120, 122-123, 127, 131, 133, 137, 144-147, 151
Leadership paradigms, 109-111
Learning, 18, 20, 28, 62, 85, 133, 143
Lee, General, 134-135
Lenin, 69
Levi-Strauss, 36
Lincoln, Abraham, 23, 56, 81
Linzey PIE Cycle, 115-116
Listen, 9, 28, 31, 54, 77, 80, 99, 114-115, 144
Lombardi, Vince, 70
Love, 1, 3, 5, 16, 42, 69-70, 128
Loyalty, 3, 34, 37, 39, 41, 48, 51, 55, 62, 70, 85-87, 90, ,93-94, 105, 134
Lukes, Steven, 60-61
Lynch, Robert Porter, 130

MacArthur, Douglass, 69-70, 91, 122
Madison, James, 7, 12, 92
Manipulation, 61
Manson, Charles, 2
Massachusetts Bay Colony, 5
Matrices, 96-97, 101
Matrix, 101-104
McDaniel, Doug, 62
Mediocrity, 32, 37
Mentor, xx, 77-79, 96, 109, 136
Mentoring, 73, 79, 109
Microsoft, 26
Military, 26, 51, 57, 90, 126-127, 131, 136
Military chaplains, 123
Mirrors, 125
Mission, 44, 50, 66, 70, 72-75, 77, 79, 106, 108, 111, 115, 127, 136, 151
Mission Control, 66-67

161

Subject Index

Mission Statement, 74, 78–79
Model, 7–9, 33, 36–37, 59, 75, 77–79, 88, 90, 92, 94–95, 109–112, 124
Moderation, 30
Money, 23, 33, 57, 62, 91, 94, 97, 108, 127, 130
Montagner, Hubert, 68
Montgomery and Ward, 42
Montgomery, Field Marshall, 70, 122
Moral absolutes, 21–22
Moral code, 11–12, 16
Moral dilemmas, 37
Moral duty, 46
Moral laws, 20, 89
Moral leadership, 1–12, 19–20, 53, 56, 89, 123, 133, 145
Moral principles, 1
Morale, 77, 87
Morals, 105
Morality, 2–4, 6–7, 9–14, 16, 19–20, 32, 54, 81, 90, 133
Motivate, 54, 114, 144
Motivation, 6, 60, 70, 73, 76, 143
Muggeridge, Malcolm 124
Muse, Dr. Stephen, 123

Natural law, 1
Needs, 25, 29–30, 32, 35, 42, 48–49, 51–52, 69, 86–87, 109, 112, 114, 136, 141, 144
Negative thinker, 66–67
New Testament, 14
Nietzsche, Frederich, 58
Nine Leadership Beatitudes, 140–141
Nine Leadership Traits, 21–71
Nixon, 4
Nobel Prize, 44

O'Toole, James, 84
Old Testament, 14–15
Ong, Walter, 124
Open-minded, 99

Operation of group dynamics, 57
Optimist, 64, 65, 87, 143
Organize, 100, 126–127
Organizational Conflict, 121–122
Oxford Dictionary, 19

Paradigms, 109–111
Passive negative, 4
Passive positive, 4
Patience, 31, 49–50, 94
Peace of mind, 6
Peace, 34, 53–54, 141
Peacemaker, 54
Peale, Norman Vincent, 67
Peer pressure, 30
Perseverance, 49–52, 134, 143
Personal Mission Statement, 149, 151
Personal Vision Statement, 149–151
Personality ethic, xviii–xix
Perspective, 67, 119, 126–127, 150
Persuasion, 57, 61–62, 126–127
Peter, the Apostle, 94–95
PIE (Plan, Implement, Evaluate), 74
Plan, 39, 51, 67, 109, 116–117, 125, 134
Plato, 5
Point of view, 42, 60
Political campaigns, 34
Politics, 57, 98
Porter, Michael E., 25
Position, 17, 23, 25, 46, 52, 54, 57–58, 62, 80, 82, 111, 126, 144–145
Positive thinkers, 65–67
Positive thinking, 38, 67, 142
Possibility thinking, 63–65, 67
Power positions, 72
Power, 10, 12, 19, 23, 28–29, 38, 40, 52–53, 56–61, 63, 65, 70, 85, 91, 106, 133, 149
Power, Types and Sources, 57–58
   Charisma, personal or group, 57
   Delegated authority, 57
   Expertise, ability, or skills, 57

Subject Index

Force, 57
Influence or tradition, 57
Knowledge, 57
Money, 57
Operation of group dynamics, 58
Persuasion, 57
Social class or position, 57
PowerPoint, 128
Presentation, 125, 128, 130–131
Preston, Sandra, 74
Principles, xi–xii, xx, 8, 10, 17, 20, 34, 46, 73, 76–79, 82, 91–92, 105, 137, 141, 151
Priorities, 70, 122, 134, 144
Problems, 28, 37, 47, 50, 63–65, 67, 76, 79–80, 82–83, 86, 98, 107, 135, 141–142
Productivity, 7, 9, 39, 41, 44, 46, 111, 143
Public speaking, 124, 127, 129, 132, 147
Purpose, 8–9, 24, 39, 50, 75, 82, 92, 98, 124, 126, 128, 134, 136
Pyramid of Success, 93

Quality time, 112

Rational choice, 58–59
Reagan, 4
Regulations, 78, 97
Relationships, xii, xx, 14, 16–17, 23, 25, 32–34, 52, 55, 63, 69, 73, 78–79, 88, 94, 96, 100–101, 108, 111–115, 118, 122, 129, 136, 142–143
Relationship dynamics, 79, 112–113
Relationship Dynamics Wheel, 112–113
Relativism, 21–22
Reliability, 48, 62, 83, 94
Religion, 19, 57
Religious, 5, 14, 17, 19–20, 22, 24, 61, 118–120, 126, 135, 137
Research, 48, 74, 126–130
Resolution, 24, 131

Respect, 9, 33, 36, 42–46, 52, 63, 69, 71, 81, 85, 92, 94, 99, 105, 126–127, 135, 140–141, 143, 146
Responsibility, 5–6, 8, 17, 29, 48, 51, 70, 74–75, 77, 92, 99–100, 106, 109, 122, 134–135, 147
Reynolds, Erin DeMeester, 124
Risk, 18, 26, 65, 97, 114, 142
Roosevelt, Franklin D., 69
Roosevelts (both), 4
Rules, 14, 17, 32, 56, 97, 99, 129, 151
Rusoff, Jane Wollman, 62

Schuller, Robert, 66
Schwarzkopf, General Norman, 69–70, 89
Secular, 20, 61, 119–120, 135
Self-advancement, 53
Self-confidence, 28, 52, 54–55, 92, 132
Self-control, 29–31, 35, 94
Self-discipline, 29–31, 51, 134
Self-esteem, 48, 54–55
Self-fulfilling prophecy, 47–48
Self-image, 33
Selflessness, 24, 33, 52, 81, 87
Self-respect, 33
Self-starters, 51
Senge, Peter, 40
Sensitive, 53, 55, 80, 114
Serenity, 52
Servanthood, xvii, 54, 74, 87, 108, 111–112
Serve, 18, 63, 108–109, 118, 136
Service, 25, 65, 67, 90, 94, 105
Seven Guidelines for a Consensus, 98
Share, 17, 40, 63, 78, 115, 126, 130
Shared values, 2, 19, 39
Shared vision, 39–40
Skills, 39, 49, 51, 56–57, 74–75, 77, 79, 86, 92, 94, 108, 111–112, 131, 133, 142, 147
Sloan, Alfred, 70, 122
Small groups, 136

Subject Index

Smart, Bradford D., 37
Smith, Barrett, 118, 120
Smith, Fred, 51
Social class, 57
Soviet Union, 4
Speakers, 125–127, 129–130
Spheres of influence, xi, xvii, xix–xx, 112
Spiritual, 19–20, 76, 136–137, 142, 147
Spiritual constitution, 11
Spiritual heritage, 5
Spiritual insight, 10
Spiritual lives, 6
Stability, 52
Standards, 6, 14, 16, 20, 22, 34, 46, 70, 75–76, 81, 85
Steadfastness, 134
Stories, 126–127
Strategic, 38–39, 60
Strategy, 67, 69
Subordinates, 99, 107–112, 118–120, 134, 141
Supervising, 76–77
Supervisory Advice to Leaders, 80
Supervisory leadership, 80
Support, 7, 17, 19, 26, 29, 34, 45, 63, 72, 79, 96, 100, 126–127
Swenson, Mike, 62

Tact, 87–88
Taft, 4
Team Building's Ten Commandments, 100–101
Team leadership, 96
Teamwork, 26, 70, 75, 77–78, 96, 106, 111–115, 147
Technical formation, 75–76, 78
Techniques, 7, 9, 73, 92, 124, 132–133, 149
Temperance, 29
Ten Commandments, xi, xxi, 5, 12–18, 100
Ten Team Building Rules, 99–100
Thatcher, Margaret, 4–5, 82

Theories of Power, 58
Theresa, Mother, 124
Tjosvold, Dean and Mary, 25
Tolerance, 33, 43, 49
Tools, xi–xii, xviii, xx, 73, 79, 88, 125
Toughness, 52, 70, 80
Tradition, 22, 57, 109–110, 118, 136–137
Traditional morality, 3
Training, 75–79, 85, 90, 106, 108, 112, 123, 131
Trait, 2, 8, 17, 21–24, 29, 36, 43, 48, 52–53, 63, 68–72, 78–80, 85, 92–95, 145, 147, 150–151
Truman, Harry, 4, 78
Trust, 4, 19, 28, 33–35, 37, 44–46, 48–49, 51, 63, 66, 70, 77, 79, 81, 83, 85, 94, 111, 114, 118, 120–121, 130–131, 134–136, 143–144, 146–147
Trustworthy, 17, 32, 34, 48–49, 143, 145–146
Truth, 3–4, 14, 33–34, 45, 49, 59, 89, 98, 105, 137
Truthful, 34–35, 115
Truthfulness, 115
Tutu, Desmond, 44–45
Twelve Habits of Effective Leaders, 73, 80–88
Twelve Principles of Job Leadership, 76–78
Tyranny, 6

U.S. Constitution, 90, 92
U.S. Military, 127
U.S. Military Academy, 91
Unconditional acceptance, 135, 137–140
Unconditionally, 22, 137–138
Understanding, 20, 43, 75, 86, 90, 114, 120–121, 130, 132, 145
Unilateral decisions, 99
United States, 4–5, 7, 11–12, 24
Universals, 1

Subject Index

Values, 2, 3, 19, 23–24, 29, 34, 36, 61, 75, 82, 84–86, 89–91, 94–95, 102–105, 122, 135, 141, 144, 150
Verify, 7, 74
Versatility, 131
Vision Quest, 40
Vision, 7–8, 18–19, 22, 25, 38–42, 50, 67, 82–83, 85, 87–88, 92, 100, 107, 121, 134
Volunteers, 24, 73, 77, 109, 118, 150
Voting, 81, 97, 99, 119

Walesa, Lech, 144

Wall Street Journal, 10, 145
Wal-Mart, 26
Walters, Barbara, 70
Walton, Clarence, 89
Warsaw Pact, 9
Washington, George, 13
Western culture, 137
Western European Nations, 9
Western life, 6
Winthrop, John, 5
Wisdom, 7, 20, 54, 133
Wooden, John, 68, 93–94, 146
Wright Brothers, 67

www.ingramcontent.com/pod-product-compliance
Lightning Source LLC
Chambersburg PA
CBHW050806160426
43192CB00010B/1666